FILL OF JOY:

MORE TALES FROM MONTLAKE FILL

BY CONSTANCE SIDLES

Constancy Press, LLC *Seattle, Washington*

Fill of Joy: More Tales from Montlake Fill
First Edition

Copyright © 2013 Constancy Press, LLC

All rights reserved. No part of this book may be reproduced in any form or by any electronic or mechanical means, including information storage and retrieval systems, without permission in writing from Constancy Press, LLC, except by a reviewer, who may quote brief passages in a review.

Note: All illustrations and photographs are used with permission from the artists and photographers, who retain their copyrights.

Published and distributed by Constancy Press, LLC
4532 48th Avenue NE
Seattle, WA 98105 USA
phone: (206)522-7513
http://www.constancypress.com

Printed in Hong Kong by Mantec Production Company
September 2013

ISBN: 978-0-9842002-2-1 $23.95

Library of Congress Control Number: 2013911451

Dedication and Acknowledgements

Although my name is the one on the cover, I could not have created this book alone. I wish to honor and give thanks to all those who helped make my dream come true—this book is dedicated to you:

To my beloved husband, John, my muse and mentor, my tech expert and funmeister;

To my editors Amy Davis, she of the eagle eye; and Cynthia White, so gloriously picky;

To the photographers, whose artistry and generosity knew no bounds: Tim Kuhn, Doug Parrott, Gregg Thompson, Tom Sanders, Katie Lloyd, Lewis Johnson, Idie Ulsh, Alex MacKenzie, Dennis Paulson, Glen Tepke, Collin Vassallo, Tom Schworer, Evan Houston, Ryan Merrill, Doug Schurman, Joe Sweeney, and Loupy Smith;

To the artists and poets, who shared their inspiration: Lisa Ravenholt, Molly Hashimoto, Hiroko Seki, Alex MacKenzie, Jim Brems, Rachel Sprague, Judith Yarrow, Jane Sandes, Carleen Zimmerman, Suzanne Peterson, Sally Yeager, Tony Parr, and Ethan Madsen;

To the librarians of the Elisabeth C. Miller Library, who were always willing to help me track down the information I needed: Rebecca Alexander, Martha Ferguson, Tracy Mehlin, Carrie Bowman, Laura Blumhagen, and Brian Thompson;

To the scientists—both professional and citizen—who provided expertise without stint: Idie Ulsh, Dennis Paulson, Merrill Peterson, and Bill Leonard;

To the faculty and staff of the University of Washington Botanic Gardens, who keep Union Bay Natural Area alive and well: Lisa Graumlich, Tom De Luca, Sarah Reichard, Fred Hoyt, Kern Ewing, David Zuckerman, and Annie Bilotta;

To all the volunteers who have worked so hard to build a boardwalk trail through Yesler Swamp, the easternmost part of the Fill, and especially to: Carol Arnold, Jean Colley, Fred Hoffer, Jerry Gettel, Rob Edsforth, Art Feinglass, and Allie Kerr:

Thank you.

Baby Pied-billed Grebe ©Tim Kuhn

Contents

Contents v
Illustrations & Photographs vii

I Winter   1
1 Dance of Life 2
2 Our Swans 9
3 Control 15
4 Join In 21
5 His Little Tuft 27
6 Common Wealth 34
7 Let This Be a Lesson 39
8 Vistas 45

II Spring   51
9   Behold, Thou Art Fair 52
10 Forever Young 58
11 A Bit of a Fwap 63
12 Étude in Gray Minor 68
13 Nuance 74
14 That's Tough 80
15 Two Elusive Dreams 87
16 Winners 93

III Summer — 101

17 Renaissance 102
18 You Kids Get Off My Lawn! 110
19 Home 116
20 Extra Ordinary 123
21 Black Magic 128
22 Oxygen 134
23 Can You Hear Me Now? 141
24 Perfection 147

IV Fall — 151

25 Treasure 152
26 Let It Go 159
27 Faith in Your Feathers 164
28 Dumb and Dumber 170
29 Airs and Graces 176
30 The Age of Dinosaurs 183
31 The Comedy Cat Won't Go in the Tragedy Bag 189
32 Ripples 195

V Appendices — 201

Map of Montlake Fill 202
A The Meaning of the Fill 204
B Birds of Montlake Fill 221
Index 237

Illustrations & Photographs

Baby Pied-billed Grebe, by Tim Kuhn	iv
Wahkiakum Lane in winter, by Alexandra MacKenzie	1
Hooded Mergansers, by Doug Parrott	4
Trumpeter Swans, by Kathrine Lloyd	8
Trumpeter Swans, by Doug Parrott	11
Song Sparrow, by Tim Kuhn	14
Virginia Rail, by Tim Kuhn	18
Muskrat, by Lewis E. Johnson	19
Black-capped Chickadee, by Tim Kuhn	22
Milbert's Tortoiseshell butterfly, by Idie Ulsh	23
Bushtit, by Tim Kuhn	25
Tufted Duck, by Collin Vassallo	28
Greater Scaup, by Doug Parrott	32
American Beaver, by Lewis E. Johnson	33
Male Common Merganser, by Gregg Thompson	36
Female Common Merganser, by Tim Kuhn	37
Pine Siskin, by Doug Parrott	40
Cooper's Hawk, by Doug Parrott	42
Mourning Cloak butterfly, by Idie Ulsh	43
Eastern Phoebe, by Ryan Merrill	46
Coyote, by Kathrine Lloyd	50
Center for Urban Horticulture garden in spring, by Lewis E. Johnson	51
Great Blue Heron, by Doug Parrott	54
Great Blue Heron stabbing, by Doug Parrott	55
Bullfrog, by Doug Parrott	57
Anna's Hummingbird, by Tim Kuhn	60
Ruby-crowned Kinglet, by Gregg Thompson	61
Double-crested Cormorants, by Doug Parrott	64
Double-crested Cormorant, by Gregg Thompson	65
Sora, by Tim Kuhn	69
Orange-crowned Warbler, by Doug Parrott	72
Say's Phoebe, by Gregg Thompson	75
Cooper's Hawk, by Tim Kuhn	79
Brewer's Blackbird, by Tim Kuhn	83
Wilson's Snipe, by Doug Parrott	89
Killdeer nest, by Evan Houston	92
American Goldfinch, by Doug Parrott	96
American Kestrel, by Thomas Sanders	97
Shoveler's Pond in summer, by Mary Lou Smith	101
American Robin, by Tim Kuhn	104
Cinnabar Moth, by Doug Parrott	109
Pied-billed Grebe chick, by Doug Parrott	112
Northern Flicker chicks, by Doug Parrott	117
Red-eared Slider, by Kathrine Lloyd	121

Mallard, by Doug Parrott 124
Black Swift, by Glen Tepke 129
Cliff Swallow, by Tim Kuhn 133
Marsh Wren, by Doug Parrott 136
Marsh Wren building a nest, by Doug Parrott 139
Common Yellowthroat, by Thomas Sanders 143
Barn Swallow, by Doug Parrott 150
Southwest Pond in fall, by Lewis E. Johnson 151
Long-billed Dowitcher, by Gregg Thompson 155
Northern Shoveler, by Tim Kuhn 158
Belted Kingfisher, by Thomas Sanders 162
Merlin, by Doug Parrott 166
Killdeer, by Kathrine Lloyd 167
Turkey Vulture, by Tim Kuhn 171
Western Grebe, by Doug Parrott 179
Least Sandpiper, by Kathrine Lloyd 182
Red-winged Blackbird, by Doug Parrott 187
Barred Owl, by Doug Parrott 190
Eight-spotted Skimmer, by Dennis Paulson 194
American Coots, by Doug Parrott 198
American Wigeon, by Doug Schurman 199
Green Heron, by Thomas Sanders 201
Map of Montlake Fill 202
Red-necked Phalarope, by Kathrine Lloyd 205
"Flight", by Thomas Schworer 206
"Reverence", by Lisa Ravenholt 207
Turkey Vulture number story, by Ethan Madsen 208
Main Pond in summer, by Mary Lou Smith 209
Common Yellowthroat, by Alexandra MacKenzie 210
Wood Duck, by Molly Hashimoto 211
Shoveler's Pond, Winter, by Sarah T. Yeager 212
Dragonfly, by Hiroko Seki 213
Buffleheads, by Tony Parr 214
Bald Eagle and Osprey, by Jane Sandes 215
Shoveler's Pond, by Suzanne E. Peterson 216
Union Bay Natural Area, by Carleen Ormbrek Zimmerman 219
"Bird Stone", by James Brems 220
Canvasback, by Doug Parrott 222
Dunlin, by Doug Parrott 227
Chipping Sparrow, by Joe Sweeney 231
Great Blue Heron, by Doug Parrott 236

Artists' and Photographers' Websites

Molly Hashimoto . . . . `http://www.mollyhashimoto.com`
Tim Kuhn . . . . `http://timkuhnphotography.zenfolio.com`
Kathrine Lloyd . . . . `http://9livesimages.com`
Alexandra MacKenzie . . . . `http://mizmak.blogspot.com`
Jane Sandes . . . . `http://janesandes.com`
Thomas Schworer . . . . `http://www.thomasschworer.com`
Hiroko Seki . . . . `http://www.hirokoseki.com`
Glen Tepke . . . . `http://www.pbase.com/gtepke`
Carleen Ormbrek Zimmerman `http://seattle.urbansketchers.org`

Part I
Winter

1. Dance of Life

Hooded Mergansers in winter are very busy ducks. If they're not diving for fish in the shallow coves and ponds of the Fill, the males are preening their feathers so they can look gorgeous for the females. Each brown, white, and black feather must be in perfect condition in perfect place so the males can put on a perfect display. It's the only way to secure a mate, a result profoundly to be wished for, if you're a duck.

Hooded Mergansers are serial monogamists and believe in moving on after each one-year collaboration. This can be a great strategy if you want to spread your genes far and wide, but it also means you've got to start from scratch every year.

In the race to win a mate, it's a great advantage to be first on base, as it were, so the males get into breeding plumage as fast as they can. Unfortunately, impressing females is a dangerous game, because the male who stands out in the females' eyes can also be uncomfortably noticeable to predators' eyes. Or as the ancient Greek philosophers used to say, your greatest strength is also your greatest weakness.

As far as I can tell, the male mergansers don't seem to be worried much by the danger, though. The ones on Main Pond preen right out in the open, despite the fact that Cooper's Hawks infest the Fill and are known to plunge into water after tasty ducks from time to time. I guess mergansers take the Alfred E. Neuman approach to philosophy. Neuman, you may recall, was the jug-eared cover boy of *Mad* magazine, whose motto was, "What, me worry?"

Once the males are done preening, they all stampede to the nearest pond to find a likely looking female to commence impressing.

First the males extend their necks like E.T. phoning home. Then they point their bills to the sky and touch their heads to their backs, executing a move that would make any circus contortionist writhe with envy. But the mergansers don't even break a sweat. I suppose it's part of their strategy. They want to make their moves look easy so their rivals will be cowed and the females will take note.

But the females don't take note. At least not at first. They studiously ignore all the frantic males posturing before their eyes. Eventually, of course, the females will make their selections, and thus the dance of life continues.

It is our dance, too, as you can see for yourself at any singles bar on the planet. I know this from personal experience, due to an incident that happened when my husband and I were living briefly in exile in Los Angeles. I had just given birth to our first child, and my mother came down from Seattle to help out. One day, when it was my husband's turn to stay home with the baby, my mother took me aside and told me she had always wanted to check out the legendary L.A. bar scene. "And now is my chance," she whispered. "Where can we go?"

I had no clue. Even in my greenest salad days, I had avoided singles bars, on the theory that I was unlikely to meet a fellow birder in one. Now here was my mother, panting to go. Against my better judgment, I called the only socialite I knew to ask for a recommendation. She suggested a bar in Venice Beach, near Gold's Gym, the famous bodybuilders' gym where Arnold Schwarzenegger used to work out. My mother was enthusiastic. I think she had a secret crush on Arnold and hoped he might pay a visit to his old haunts. In any case, we went, me in my dowdy post-maternity dress, she as dolled up as any 67-year-old grandma with fallen arches can get.

The bar consisted of a sunken pit—which was the dance floor—encircled by a ring of tiny tables and chairs. The tables were occupied by women pretending to talk about the serious issues of the day while they drank their cocktails and ignored the men who were posturing down below in the pit. Rock music was throbbing in the air. No one was dancing.

Hooded Merganser males impressing a female © Doug Parrott

My mother headed for the one unoccupied table in the house and managed to secure it by scooping aside two statuesque blonds who were racing to grab the table but had made the mistake of wearing giant platform heels. Mom was in her running shoes and carried her signature red leather bag, an outsized accessory that served as her purse, pillow, bank vault, shopping bag, and cowcatcher. The blonds didn't stand a chance.

Once seated, my mother signaled for a waiter to bring us some drinks. "This is fun," she gushed. "Everyone is so young and alive."

She wasn't exaggerating. The place was packed with young people, all apparently single. I think my mom and I were the only married women in the joint. Not that this hampered my mother. While I was busy taking in the human circus and thinking how duck-like it was, she was busy trying to catch the eye of hunky guys in the pit. I found this out when two men looked over at our table and whistled at her.

It took me right back to my teenage years, when my parents were constantly doing things to mortify us kids. "Mom," I hissed, "you're a married woman!"

"I know," she said out of the corner of her mouth, "but they're so sexy. Don't you think?"

It was at this moment I became fully adult, admitted into the union of women that I had always suspected existed but had never been allowed to join. When I was a little girl, I used to crawl under the kitchen table to eavesdrop on the gossip my mother shared with her women friends. It was like a club. The women would all sit around drinking coffee, talking about the challenges of their lives: their children, their poverty, husbands who were good men but by no means perfect, love that was good but by no means perfect either. I understood very little but drank it in as avidly as I did the sips of coffee I would sneak when I thought no one was looking.

My mother was almost a mythic figure to me then, bigger, stronger, wiser than I could possibly imagine. She loomed large in my life even after I left home, a parental figure always there to help, to advise, to criticize, to judge.

We were not friends because we were not equals. Until that moment in the L.A. bar when she shared her admiration and her lust for those beautiful young men on the dance floor. They *were* good to look at, and although she and I were both married, both mothers, both faithful to our husbands, we were also both women. Together. We were connected in a way we had never felt before, not just by emotion but by a sense of union with all women that extended far back into the formless mists of time, and far forward into the unseeable future.

That moment of shared adulthood and female bonding was brief. Unknown to us then, my mom was already doomed, riddled with the cancer that was to kill her soon, the cancer that completed our dance, that turned her into the child and me into the caregiver. Oh, treasure that fleeting moment of connection, if it should ever come to you. Treasure all such moments of joy, no matter how brief, for they can give you a lifetime of memories that will fill your heart.

This lesson for me was articulated by a book of short stories I read around the same time as my mother's visit. I can't remember the name of the book anymore, but I will never forget one of the stories. It concerned a prince and princess who were deeply in love. So great was their love, in fact, that it transcended time and space, spreading goodness and light to all who witnessed it. All, that is, except for an evil witch, who wanted the young man for herself. One day, disguised as a beautiful woman, the old witch approached the prince when he was hunting alone in the forest. She offered herself to him, but he rejected her. "I love another," he said simply.

"Then, since you refuse my love, you shall know my wrath," the witch cried, turning herself back into the ugly hag she really was, both inside and out. "Never shall you be with your love again," saying which, she turned the prince into a panther who hunted by night and was human by day, and the princess into a falcon who flew in the day and could be human only at night.

But the fabric of magic that weaves through the world quivered at such malice and called on the other magicians of the world to intervene. "Take heart," the magicians said to the stricken prince.

"Nothing can keep you forever from your wife, for love is stronger than hate." And they fought the witch. They could not stop her from transforming the prince into a panther of the moonlight nor the princess into a falcon of the bright day, but for one brief moment at dawn and again at dusk, when both the Moon and the Sun rule the heavens together, the panther became man, the falcon woman, and the two lovers could love again.

Of course, since this is a fairy tale, the lovers eventually figured out a way to defeat the evil witch, regain their proper forms, and live happily ever after. I don't even remember exactly how they did it. Maybe it involved a random act of kindness to a powerful wizard, kind of like buying a stranger a latte and asking the stranger to pass it forward. Or it might have involved overcoming seemingly insurmountable obstacles, like fixing two flat tires that you got on the same trip because your husband told you the tires were bald but you didn't listen.

Anyway, that's not my point. Happy endings may be heartwarming, but they are also humdrum, at least insofar as fiction is concerned. They can't teach you anything, because they don't reflect any known reality. The fact is, there are no real endings at all, as long as life itself continues. There are only more steps to walk, more corners to look around, more adventures to undertake.

Rather than focus on a fictional happy ending, I'm far more intrigued by the heart of the story, the part that teaches us to savor the moment. For the day is beautiful, but so is the night. The dawn is full of hope and promise, the twilight full of memory.

We must embrace each time that comes to us in life, because each gives us an opportunity to construct our own stage whereon we can dance our songs of joy.

"Our" three Trumpeter Swans on Union Bay ©Kathrine Lloyd

2. Our Swans

In December 2008, Seattle was hit by a historically heavy snowstorm. The city ground to a halt, as it always does whenever the snow flies. In such cases, there is only one response a birder can make: I went to the Fill to see what the storm had driven in.

As I reached the Lone Pine Tree on the Loop Trail, the highest point of the Fill, I saw what looked like a collection of small, white icebergs bobbing on the pewter-gray waters of Union Bay. A flock of fifteen Trumpeter Swans had come down from their wintering grounds on the Skagit floodplain, seeking food. They must have liked the unlimited fodder they found in Lake Washington, for eleven of them stayed all winter.

Among the adult swans were three juveniles. It's easy to tell juvenile Trumpeter Swans apart from the snow-white adults because juveniles' feathers are gray. They don't molt into their all-white plumage until spring.

Throughout that winter, the three juveniles floated together on the lake, sometimes coming close to shore on Water Lily Cove, sometimes coasting all the way over to the Marina at Conibear. At first, their parents stayed nearby, but as the juveniles grew more skilled at being swans, the parents drifted off, leaving the kids to fend for themselves. This the juveniles did well, taking turns dipping their long necks into the water to pull up plants while one sibling kept a wary eye out for boaters. At night, the three would paddle to a log that was stuck at the entrance of Yesler Cove. There, they would preen until the Sun dipped below the horizon and the lambent light of evening drew on. Under cover of darkness, the swans would slip into the cove to sleep. No matter where they were either night or day, though, they would always stay close together, tootling softly, and often touching each other gently with their bills.

When spring arrived with its siren song tempting all the swans north, the juveniles felt restless. The Far North was calling to them, too. One night, they skimmed along the water's surface with wings outspread, running faster and faster until they were airborne. Then, trumpeting to each other to stay together, they joined the vast river of swans and geese migrating to the tundra to breed. In the morning, I looked for them in vain. Gone. Oh, how bereft was the bay, and we who were left behind.

The next November, I began to scan the lake every day for our swans, hoping they had made it through the spring and summer, hoping they would remember their winter home, hoping they would come back to us. In late December, they did! By now, they were snow-white and looked like all the other swans who come to our state every year to feed and grow fat. The three who showed up at Union Bay, though, were special. They always swam close together, tootling softly in a song only they could understand. Often they touched each other gently with their bills. I was sure they were "our" swans, who had come back to the home where they had grown up so happily together.

All winter long, you could find our swans somewhere on the lake near Montlake Fill. In the spring, they got restless again as they felt the call to go north to the tundra. One day I looked for them, but the lake was empty. They were gone, once again leaving us behind to yearn for their return.

I have felt this hole in my heart before. It first occurred when my oldest son, just seventeen and barely out of high school, departed on a years-long excursion to the Outer Islands of Micronesia. Alex wanted no part of a humdrum existence, eking out a living in the safety of a city. He longed for adventure. When he left with only a gym bag, I smiled and waved at his departing back. Then I went to the Fill and cried.

Trumpeter adult with two gray juveniles © Doug Parrott

I did the same thing when my youngest son left for college. He and my husband elected to make a father-son road trip out of the journey. I watched while Nathan packed our little Honda Civic so tightly I wasn't sure the doors would close. "Your brother took only a gym bag when he left," I said. Eyeing the potted Spathiphyllum lily (nicknamed Plantus) that Nathan was placing on the last remaining space in the back seat, I added, "I don't think all your stuff is going to fit."

"Don't worry," he assured me. "I've planned everything very carefully." Leaning upon the open door, he managed to close it, fitting the protruding door handle perfectly into a little space he had carved in the wall of his possessions in the back. "See?"

Just then, his father came out, dragging a huge suitcase. "Where do you want me to put my bag?" he asked.

Somehow they managed to find room, although the car grew so heavy the tail pipe dragged on the cement when they eased out of the driveway. I smiled and waved at their departing backs. Then I went to the Fill and cried.

I cried when my daughter left for college, laughed when she moved back home, and cried again when she found her own apartment. "For Pete's sake," my husband said, "she's living only a few miles away."

"I know," I wept. "I'm going to the Fill."

It is hard to be a human parent. When the swan children leave home, the parents go with them. Everyone stays together, at least until they reach the breeding grounds. But we human parents have no wings to fly, and we're not supposed to follow our grown children when they leave the nest. Our role is to wave them off with a smile and wait, hoping they will return home again some day. American families often scatter to the winds. It has come to seem natural, but still I miss my children when they go off on their adventures, adults though they may be, leaving me behind, unable to follow them except in my mind's eye, just as I do with the swans.

When November rolled around again, I looked for our swans but could not find them. Days went by, and our swans did not return.

Birders reported swans arriving everywhere in the Skagit, but Union Bay remained empty. December came and still no swans. I began to think our babies had gone their separate ways, as kids so often do. But then on January 1 of the New Year, I looked across the bay and saw two swans. As I watched, four more flew in to join the pair.

They all swam around each other, paddling in stately fashion as only swans can. Then three snow-white swans drew close together and gently touched each other with their bills. Our babies were back, and they had brought their spouses! Oh, indescribable joy.

The six swans stayed with us all winter, now in pairs, now in threes. When spring came, they heard the call of the Far North again and answered it, as swans must. Now that winter has returned, so have my hopes. Day after day, I have looked for them. Yesterday, as I was walking in Yesler Swamp, I heard their unmistakable trumpeting. I scanned the sky but couldn't find them. Like a mom peering at all the faces of airplane passengers in the terminal, I looked at every bird. Nothing. But I knew. I knew.

Hurrying as fast as I could, I rushed over to East Point, where I could scan the entire lake. There, at the entrance to Water Lily Cove were two swans, making a heart shape with their necks. As I watched, more swans flew in: four, then seven, then more, until eighteen swans graced our bay. Among them were four gray juveniles. I sighed a great sigh of joy.

I can no longer tell our swans apart from all the others. I suspect one of the parents of the four juveniles is ours, but both adults are way too busy to take time out to gossip with their siblings. They need to shepherd the kids around the bay, making sure they eat, watching out for danger, teaching them how to be swans.

Eventually, these newly born youngsters will grow up and fly away, as their parents did. The Far North will call to them, and they will answer. But if the swans cannot stay here always, they can always return, as children do now and then, bringing their partners, thrilling all of us members of their extended family with their beauty.

With their being.

Song Sparrow © Tim Kuhn

3. Control

Of all the challenging weather conditions that make birders' lives difficult, fog may very well be at the top of the list. Not only does fog cut visibility down to near zero, it makes songbirds hunker down and hide from view. Even if we could find them, we wouldn't be able to identify them, because the dimness of the light turns all colors to murky gray, making every bird a nondescript, dark lump (or a dot, depending on the size of the bird and its distance).

But fog at the Fill is one of the most magical of all phenomena. It muffles the sounds of the city and lets the wild speak softly.

Today I was down at the Turtle Logs, peering through thick shrouds of fog and trying to make out ducks on the lake when I heard a Song Sparrow burble out a most beautiful song. I thought the bird was 20 or 30 meters away because the song was so soft. But by chance I looked up, and there he was, only one foot away from me. Not afraid. We eyed each other for a moment, and then he broke into his softly modulated song again. I could see every feather of his throat quiver with the effort. Singing soft is much harder than singing loud, as any opera star will tell you.

The notes of his song trickled into the quiet, slowly filling the cathedral of the cottonwood grove until there didn't seem to be room for any other sound. All the other birds fell silent, until only the Song Sparrow's voice echoed in the glade, rising to the treetops, falling to the path below, winding around every leaf and blade of grass in a chorus of pure beauty.

I have been following the career of this singer, ever since he made his debut on the blackberry bush that persistently eludes the gardeners trying to eradicate all the invasive plants that crowd out the natives here. His audition was not an auspicious one, more a series of grunts than soaring notes. No doubt Simon Cowell, the curmudgeonly judge of *Britain's Got Talent* fame, would have ruthlessly pressed the big white X, eliminating the singer from the competition. I, however, heard something in that little bird's voice that I thought might develop into greatness. "Keep going," I said encouragingly. And he did. Every day, he would pop out of his bush when I walked by and sing a little phrase. Gradually, he got better. And now this, this song of songs, this triumph of lyricism.

When he was done with his aria, I wanted to respond in kind, but unfortunately, a dreadful song had got stuck in my brain—you know how that is—and I couldn't call anything else to mind. I started in, regardless. "O-o-o-ok-la-homa, where the wind comes sweeping down the...." I had to stop. It was just too pathetic. "You sing, then," I told the bird. I make a much better audience than performer, and he was no kind of audience at all, so we were both satisfied.

I never know exactly where I rate on the weirdness scale of human behavior, although I suspect I'm way out on the narrow end of the bell curve. I probably fall a little more into the average distribution of the curve if you count only the subset of birders, but even there, I'm nearly off the scale. So I guess it won't change my stats any if I admit that I do talk to birds. Oh, not like my Aunt Fanny, who owned a yellow parakeet to whom she would coo, "Pretty bird, pretty bird, who's a pretty bird?" and then feed him a seed held between her teeth. The birds of the Fill are not pets and would probably peck off my lips if I tried that trick on them.

No, I speak to birds as fellow creatures of the wild planet I too inhabit. Not as equals, exactly, nor colleagues. Fellow travelers perhaps. I speak to birds because we humans are made for speech. We communicate principally by talking, even when the communication is unwanted, unnecessary, impossible for others to comprehend.

The birds I talk to hear me, but they cannot understand me. I do not expect them to. I talk to them because with us humans, to think is to speak, to feel is to speak, and I think and feel deeply at the Fill.

Maybe it's a conceit, but I believe the birds like to hear me talk. It reassures them that I am going to stay in my portion of the Fill, meaning, not just on the trail but in the tamed part of the world, leaving the wild part to them. Birds observe us closely, after all, more closely than we observe them. They have to: We are predators, we eat birds, and they are right to be wary. Many times I walk through the Fill and see vast areas of grass and trees without a bird in sight. I know the birds are present, but they hide. Often this happens because a raptor is nearby, just waiting for a clueless songbird to come out and become dinner. But many times the birds skulk under cover for no reason I can tell. When they do, I know they watch me pass by their hidden places. They remember me: my blue floppy hat, my halting step, my voice. Sometimes they sing or chip a little as I get near. I like to think it's their way of acknowledging me, of letting me know that they are here, too.

On the east side of Southwest Pond, where the Loop Trail bends closest to the shore, there is a patch of cattails where a pair of Virginia Rails have nested each spring for several years. One day, I was standing on the trail, shooting the breeze with another birder while we idly watched a Muskrat cross the pond. We talked for more than ten minutes, trading stories about birds we had seen and others we had missed. I've had hundreds of conversations like this at the Fill. All of a sudden, a Virginia Rail stalked out from behind the reeds. Cautiously, it placed one long-toed foot in front of the other. My friend and I froze into immobility, afraid we would flush this most elusive of birds. We didn't even breathe for fear the motion of our chests would frighten off the rail. Slowly, the bird paraded by, almost at our feet, waded chest-deep into a little inlet of pond water, then passed back into the reeds and disappeared.

"I think that rail heard us talking and figured we weren't paying attention to birds, so it would be okay to come out into the open," I whispered to my companion.

Since then, I've advised would-be rail-watchers to stand in this very spot and converse for ten minutes. You'd be surprised how often a rail comes out to forage in the open, much to the joy of us

Virginia Rail © Tim Kuhn

birders. This year when we tried our conversational gambit, two parent rails brought out their four newly hatched chicks. The chicks resembled tiny black footballs on stilts, skittering up and down the water-drenched verge as though they had been set into motion by an off-side kicker trying to fool the home team.

This method of soothing birds so they feel comfortable in the open is far different from tricking them to come out by playing tapes of their songs or imitating their calls. I know it's accepted practice amongst birders to lure birds into view in this way. We even have a Birder's Code of Ethics that says it's okay to play tapes or imitate calls, as long as it's done in moderation. I guess it doesn't hurt the birds, at least not much. But that's not why I gave up doing it. I quit because I didn't like the idea that I was bending wild creatures to my will. I'm not out in the wild to bend anything to my will, but rather to fit myself into a world that is very different from the civilized world where I spend most of my time.

In my constructed environment, I have plenty of things that bend to my will. And no, I don't mean my husband. I mean all the

Muskrat © Lewis E. Johnson

gadgets I control that are supposed to make my life easier and often do. I mean my schedule, where I list everything I need to do each day, and allow a certain amount of time for each task. Billable hours, the lawyers call this; the pioneers called it chores. I also mean the people to whom I give money so they will bring me things such as the mail, cook me meals such as takeout Chinese, drive me places in cabs or buses, entertain me, cure me, teach me.

I control so many things in my life, they're driving me crazy. Because in reality, all these things control me. My 97-year-old aunt told me once that she had been raised in the Great Depression and was taught to care for things so they would last as long as possible. None of her dishes had chips because she was careful to put them away slowly. None of her shelves had dust because she dusted everything at least once a week. The socks in her drawer were all folded so precisely they might have been rows of little soldiers on parade. Even the plastic bread bags she saved religiously were folded neatly and arranged by size in the drawer.

Aunt Marie lived alone on Whidbey Island for many years. Eventually, the time came when her health demanded that she move to an assisted-living facility in Seattle. She asked me to help her downsize from a three-bedroom house to a one-bedroom apartment. As a former technical writer who used to write manuals describing how to put Boeing airplanes together, she had gone about the task systematically. She got a floor plan of her apartment and figured out exactly how much furniture would fit and where it would go. Then she had to decide which of the thousands of her possessions she would take with her, and which ones she would give away. As we sorted through a lifetime of objects, the mound of giveaways grew exponentially. The pile of keepers was small.

After we were done, Aunt Marie looked at the few things she deemed essential, and the many that didn't matter. "I have spent years of my life looking after this stuff," she said, ticking off the amount of time she had always devoted to housework, car care, clothing, and tools. "Maybe I should have been more careless."

Or wilder. Like the birds. Free.

4. Join In

Though Black-capped Chickadees are among the most common birds of Montlake Fill, they are anything but commonplace. On the contrary, Black-capped Chickadees are extraordinary. Just ask yourself this: If to fix your breakfast you had to climb barefoot up a 50-foot tree, hang upside down by your toes, then drop like a trapeze artist 20 feet down to grab onto a new hold, all for the reward of one bug—and all before your first cup of coffee—how long do you think you could survive?

My answer would be three minutes, tops. Then my toes would relax their hold on my chosen branch, and I would face-plant into the mud, whereupon I would expire from embarrassment. But chickadees hang upside down to get their meals every day for years without a single complaint.

Well, maybe they complain. It's hard to say, not knowing exactly what their frequent "chickadee-dee-dee" song means.

Yesterday I was standing among the willow trees of Yesler Swamp, where the chip path curves south to the overlook on Yesler Cove, when three chickadees flew in to forage for insects. Before I knew it, they had triangulated me: one bird behind my left shoulder, one behind my right, and one in front. The one in front was so close I could see its throat throb as it gave its diagnostic call. The other two answered from concealment. The first bird examined me with its beady left eye, then shined its equally beady right eye at me. Again it spoke to its companions, and again they answered. Then everyone came out to forage.

Black-capped Chickadee © Tim Kuhn

Black-capped Chickadees are the gourmands of the avian world: They spend much of their day finding and eating food, and they aren't fussy about what they consume. They eat seeds, fruit, insects, spiders, the larvae and eggs of small arthropods, suet at feeders, and even carrion. Many of the seeds they eat are from caches they made back in October, when food was plentiful. Chickadees can remember where they have hidden all their seeds because each fall, they grow new neurons in their brains, just for this purpose. It's an enviable ability. If only I could grow a similar set of neurons to remember where I cached my car in the mall parking lot, think how much time I would save!

Bushtits soon joined the trio of chickadees, along with two Golden-crowned Kinglets, several Ruby-crowned Kinglets showing off their ruby crowns, a couple of Song Sparrows, and a Downy Woodpecker. Even the tiny Pacific Wren, who is usually so elusive I hear him but rarely see more than a flash of cinnamon brown, perched boldly on a fallen log and cocked his head at me.

The birds moved all around me as they hunted for food. Each one paid just as little or as much attention to me as it did to the other birds, and so I became part of the feeding flock. It was enchanting to be included as just one more avian among friends. Big Bird indeed.

The purpose of the flock was to find enough food to keep all of us warm on this winter day, as well as to keep us fueled throughout the long winter night to come. So we all looked for fodder, including

Milbert's Tortoiseshell butterfly © Idie Ulsh

me. Some of us searched for bugs on the undersides of leaves and branches. Some scrambled through the leaf litter looking for seeds. Some banged away on dead wood, pausing to listen a while for insect movement. I turned over a few rocks in hopes of uncovering some tasty grubs.

Despite the fact that the day was as cold as Seattle ever gets, we found abundant bugs both flying and lurking. We also had no trouble locating a goodly supply of seeds left over from the fall cornucopia. I wanted so much to join in the feast and eat the treasures I had found, but I'm not fond of invertebrates, and the seeds all around me were better left to the birds. I grew hungrier and hungrier. The thought of a cheeseburger began to take over my mind. When the flock finally moved on, so did I: they to the next patch of brush, I to the nearest fast-food outlet. Not good. My recommendation? If you want to join a feeding flock, bring your own healthy snacks.

Black-capped Chickadees are among the most generous of birds when it comes to allowing people to enter their world. They have let me participate in many of the important events of their lives, including a memorable courtship battle, when a boiling ball of birds decided to make my floppy hat the equivalent of a Madison Square Garden boxing ring. Chickadees often invite me to sing along with them as they travel from branch to branch, although, given my lack of musical abilities, I have never accepted their invitation. One year, two parents even allowed me to babysit the kids, letting me help keep the crows away from a nest they had built in a snag on Southwest Pond. The parents would leave me in charge while they flew off to find food to stuff into the bottomless pits their offspring resembled. Crows would cluster around, hoping to get at the nest hole, but they were too wary of me sitting there on guard. It was an honor to be trusted by the parent chickadees.

Or at least, so it seemed to me. But I am a storyteller, not a scientist. In fact, I can already hear the scientists out there snorting in disgust as they read my sentimental tripe. "Birds are generous about letting you into their lives? Hah! Birds aren't generous about anything. We scientists know altruism and generosity exist in the temporoparietal junctions of the human neocortex of the brain. Birds get by without any neocortex, so they don't have temporal or parietal lobes, much less any junction between them. In layman's terms, they aren't equipped to give a hoot about gifts of any kind."

I have to admit the scientists have a point, but so do I. My point has to do with a sermon Garrison Keillor recently described on his radio show, *A Prairie Home Companion:*

"On Sunday," Keillor said, "Pastor Liz gave the sermon on the story from the Gospel of Mark about the widow who gave her mite in the collection basket.... All of the rich people...made their lavish gifts with great display, and she dropped her little half-penny in, and Jesus recognized her and pointed her out to his apostles because the wealthy had given of their wealth but she had given of her poverty.

"'So,' Pastor Liz, preached, 'we should give what we do not have. This is the meaning of generosity. If we are depressed, we should throw a party. If we are lonely, we should invite people over and try to give them a good time. If you feel shame and humiliation, you should write your memoir. Give what you do not have.'"

Bushtit © Tim Kuhn

Black-capped Chickadees utterly lack humanity, but that is what they gave me: the very human gift of generosity. They are not the only ones to so gift me.

After my father died, I went to his apartment to sort through his things. My father had been poor all his life, depleted by the struggle to raise four children on the low salary that a guy with a tenth-grade education and no special training could muster. In retirement, he scraped by on a small pension and the little bit we kids managed to send him. He lived a no-frills life in a rented duplex, subsisting on the cheapest food he could find. He tried to keep his old car going despite the fact that rats kept eating the insulation around the wiring. He wore his Walmart clothes till they were threadbare and he couldn't hide the holes anymore.

In his apartment, I discovered he had apparently kept every piece of paper that ever entered his door, including cancelled checks that went back more than a decade. I decided I'd better go through the black garbage bags of checks to make sure I didn't throw out any that might be important. As I went through each check, I began to notice a pattern. Every month, when his little pension arrived, my father would write a check to charity. I found checks written to the Humane Society, the American Lung Association, Boy Scouts, Girl Scouts, the local hospital, homeless shelters, the Salvation Army—the list went on and on. Each check was for the same amount: $5.

I was stunned. How could a man so poor afford to give anything at all to others? He had never breathed a word of this to me. I doubt he told anyone. He just went ahead and did it.

My father died in debt, but he left his children a great legacy. His legacy wasn't money. It was the example of a man who lived his life with courage, sacrifice, hard work, and generosity. Thanks to him—and thanks to the lessons I learn every day from nature—I know that no matter how tough life gets, we *can* give what we don't have. And when we do, we receive untold gifts in return: gifts of kindness, strength, wisdom, joy, and connection.

My father was poor in the world's goods but wealthy in ways that money can't measure, for he was a man who knew how to give.

5. His Little Tuft

On those rare winter days when the Sun shines in Seattle, I like to get out to the Fill early, in time to watch the dawn slowly light up the world. If the horizon is clear, you can see the first tinge of color gleam on the top of Mount Rainier, then glide gently down its snowy sides in shades of pink, lavender, and gold until the entire mountain glows with unearthly light. The cold, still air of February presses down on the waters of the bay, smoothing the waves into glass, etched here and there by ducks, who leave behind only a few ripples to mark their passage.

Such a morning arrived two days ago, and at 7:00 a.m., I set up my camp stool at East Point, prepared to drink in great gulps of glory. East Point is a fine place to view the wide vista of Lake Washington, thanks in part to the ever-present beavers who have cut down the trees that used to block the sight lines here. As the sunlight grew stronger, my friend Mark Vernon shimmered into view. Mark is famous as the Long Walker Birder, a guy who thinks nothing of strolling from Montlake Fill to Volunteer Park, birding his way to heaven without the benefit of car. Mark is a very centered guy, the perfect Zen-like sort with whom to share the peace of nature.

So there we were, watching the ducks float past, watching the Sun rise higher, trading stories about birds, when, Mark reports, all of a sudden I shot up from my stool like a Polaris missile and began spouting gibberish, of which the only two words he could make out were, "Tufted Duck!"

Tufted Ducks are a kind of mussel-eating fishing duck from Siberia. They belong to the scaup family and closely resemble two

Tufted Duck in Water Lily Cove ©Collin Vassallo

of our native scaups, the Greater and the Lesser. The males of our native species have black heads and chests, gray backs, and pale flanks. They look quite similar to each other, except that Greater Scaups' heads are rounded; Lessers' heads are slightly pointy. The males of both species always seem very tailored to me, like little businessmen dressed for success. I would not be at all surprised to see one someday with a tiny briefcase tucked under a wing, waiting for the Interurban.

The Tufted Duck is different. He has a streamer of feathers sprouting from his crown and flowing down his nape. Picture a middle-aged biker with receding hairline and a mullet he has grown in order to preserve the illusion of youth, dressed in a suit because he has to appear in court for some infraction—that's the human equivalent of a Tufted Duck.

Tufted Ducks are rare at the Fill. In the past 118 years since birding records have been kept here, only one Tufted Duck has ever been seen before. Statewide, we've had only about 50 since record-keeping began. Tufted Ducks don't belong in Washington. Their true home is Asia, Europe, and Africa. Whenever a Tufted Duck appears on our shores, it means the bird has wandered far off course.

That's why, when I glanced down at the scaup paddling serenely past the point, almost within touching distance, and I saw his little tuft arch out, I literally could not believe my eyes. What I was shouting so incoherently to Mark was, "Oh my goodness, oh my goodness, oh my goodness, a Tufted Duck, oh my goodness." Because I was stuttering with excitement, it came out sounding like, "OHMAgans, OHMAgans, OHMAgans."

Mark must have thought I was chanting the latest in yoga meditation, until he realized no yogi would hop around as vigorously as I was. Then the words "Tufted Duck" smote his ears and he realized it was just a birder finding the greatest bird she had ever seen.

Since then, I've gone to East Point every morning to share the alpenglow with my little guy. As the Sun comes up, it lights the pellucid waters of the bay, turning them into liquid garnet and sapphire, then topaz. The Tufted Duck floats in the middle of this jewel case. His iridescent head feathers catch the light, now ebony, now amethyst. When he sees me, he quacks a greeting. I think I'm in love.

"Show me your tuft," I beg, and eventually, he does. He can control it, you know. Sometimes he lifts it up so it flaps behind him like a banner, every tousled feather-shaft proclaiming his beauty. Other times, he flattens it smoothly against his head. Sometimes he shakes it from side to side, like Fabio flipping his long, flowing locks.

The girl-scaups are all crazy about him. They follow him around like Justin Bieber's seventh-grade fan club, each female vying for his attention. But he is not a one-girl duck. He prefers to spread himself among his bevy, never staying too long with one. It's impossible to say whether he is only a gigolo or a serious guy who just hasn't found Mrs. Right yet.

Sometimes our resident buttoned-down male scaups paddle close to the Tufted Duck, as if to challenge him. They never pick a fight, though. I think they're hoping their beautifully tailored plumage will attract a female, but so far they have been completely ignored.

"I'm growing a mullet immediately," my husband said when I told him this story. He is making no idle threat. It's been a while since he last visited his favorite barbershop (where he can point to a photo on the wall and say, "Give me the number two," or, if he's feeling especially adventurous, "I'll take the number one"), and John's hair has grown almost Einstein-esque in its raggedy length. A barber wouldn't have any trouble at all shaping his locks into a respectable mullet.

John is not alone in this reaction. I have told several men friends about the Tufted Duck's irresistible appeal to females, and they all respond the same way. They give their heads a shake, strike a pose, and then become slightly thoughtful. I know they too are thinking about growing more hair.

Hair, you see, is a breeding "signifier" for mammals. Like a peacock's tail, it shows the male is trying. We females like to see this. If a guy puts effort into making himself beautiful—whether it's ratcheting his head up and down, up and down so fast it's a wonder it doesn't fly off, as the male Bufflehead does, or tying his Iowa-cow bow tie so all the cows' legs point properly downward, as John does—the effort proves the male is willing to make a commitment to the hard work of attracting and keeping a mate.

At the same time, a guy who is all show and nothing more raises the question, will he be helpful over the long haul? We females appreciate a good show, but if a male seems more interested in his own looks than he is in us, we know we'd better flap away immediately. For the serious business of raising kids, a prima donna simply won't do. We need a guy who will give his strength with cheerful dependability, who will be there when we need him. We want someone we can count on when we're too worn out to walk another step, lift another burden, change another diaper. We need a guy who can sit on eggs all day and keep smiling.

The dilemma for males is, what kind of plumage can possibly act as a signifier for all that?

Well, a little tuft might do. Little tufts are funny, and funny is attractive. Whenever I saw the Tufted Duck's miniature banner flapping in the breeze, I had to laugh. It looked so ridiculous. For one thing, it was just a few feathers hanging a couple inches down the bird's neck. A really serious tuft would flow over the duck's back like Superman's cape. When a passing breeze stirred it to life, it would unfurl like the mane of a lion. But you can't laugh at a lion, and Superman never made me smile.

Scientists speculate about why we humans appear to be the only species on Earth with a highly developed sense of humor. Cognitive scientist Matthew Hurley believes humor evolved to help us think. In an interview with Chris Berdik in *The Boston Globe,* Hurley says, "We're a species that thinks prodigiously. In every situation, the human brain needs to constantly anticipate the future by making assumptions about the world that unfold at breakneck speed. We do a quick and dirty assessment and make a lot of best guesses."

Unfortunately, our guesses can often be wrong. This is unpleasant, to say the least, and can lead to disaster. It is therefore crucial for us to correct our errors, reassess our assumptions, admit we were wrong. But nobody likes to to do that. We need a bribe.

"We think the pleasure of humor, the emotion of mirth, is the brain's reward for discovering its mistaken inferences," says Hurley, who got his degree from (of all places) Tufts University.

I can see Hurley's point. Few things in life offer more opportunities for goofs than do relations between mates. Thus, any spouse who can make his mate laugh is a treasure. Take the other day, for example. John and I were having one of those meaningless but heated arguments over who knows what. Couples like us who have been together for decades have these seemingly trivial discussions now and then, because all the really serious arguments were settled long ago. Not that the triviality of the argument lowers its temperature. On the contrary, I became more and more irritated with John, until finally I gave him my ultimate counterthrust: the Bug Look.

Female Greater Scaup © Doug Parrott

His Little Tuft 33

The Bug Look is one of those silent but meaningful ways we females have of expressing our thoughts about where our spouses rank on the evolutionary scale. Bugs such as cockroaches first appeared on Earth about 350 million years ago, and they haven't advanced very much since. Their IQs are tiny, their usefulness negligible, their attractiveness nonexistent. A man who gets the Bug Look from his wife has few illusions about how high he has ascended on the phylogenetic tree.

When I give John the Bug Look, it always makes him shut up. But not for long. Within a few seconds, he usually manages to summon up his humor from some deep well that for him is constantly renewed, like the magic cup that can never be emptied. This time, his response was almost instantaneous. "Well," he said, "since now I am a bug, why don't I just scuttle out to the kitchen and get you a cup of coffee?"

Something about the image of John the giant cockroach scuttling away to make coffee was so funny, I thought I was going to bust a rib. Tears of laughter ran down my face, and all discord vanished.

Laughter soothes tension, calms anger, lessens fear, leavens grief. Above all other human emotions, laughter puts life in perspective. In the face of illness, cruelty, and despair, it reminds us that we were meant to live in the light.

Laughter makes the Sun shine in our lives, and the love shine even brighter, tufts or no tufts.

American Beaver © Lewis E. Johnson

6. Common Wealth

Common Mergansers have been unusually common at the Fill this winter. Several rafts of up to 30 ducks each constantly sail around Union Bay. The ducks all have their faces underwater as they scan the depths for prey. Their foreheads push a little bow wave ahead of themselves as they paddle along. It's a welcome sight each day.

Common Mergansers are our biggest duck—the males are fish-eating powerhouses measuring more than two feet long, the females slightly smaller. When they see a tasty fish, mergansers upend themselves and give chase, driven by big webbed feet placed well back on their bodies, like giant submarine propellers.

Male Mergansers always remind me somehow of Burt Lancaster and Clark Gable. Every time I see them submerge, my brain starts running a tape it recorded unbeknownst to me at age nine from reruns of the 1958 movie, *Run Silent, Run Deep.* "Awooga! Awooga!" my relic neurons say. "Dive, dive, dive!"

I was sitting on my camp stool at the overlook near East Point one day, watching the mergansers surface nearer and nearer to shore. It is rare to see them up close, so I got very excited. That must have been what caused my quiescent neurons to spring into action.

"Up periscope!" I shouted and lifted my binoculars to my eyes, pretending I was on board the *USS Nerka* with Clark, who, I must confess, is still a major crush after all these years. When the nearest duck sank beneath the waves, I sounded my klaxon horn. "Awooga, awooga," I blared, not realizing a birder had come to stand silently behind me.

It would have been all right if I had been accompanied by a two-year-old child, maybe. You can make awooga noises if you're entertaining a toddler. But I had left such accessories at home.

The birder and I stared at each other for a paralyzed moment. "Seen anything good out there?" she asked solemnly, then burst into laughter and staggered on down the path.

I was left to gather the tattered remnants of my injured pride. "Dive, dive, dive," I muttered, but it was too late.

Luckily, the birds revived my spirits, as they always will if you let them. The male who had dived resurfaced near me. His bright eyes scanned me inquisitively. I could see his propeller feet swirling under the water. The dark green of his head feathers glistened like uncut emeralds in the weak winter sunlight. His crimson bill seemed to curve up at the edges into a little smile. "Hi there, you beauty," I breathed, back to my usual habit of talking to the birds.

Still smiling his ducky contentment that the fish were so plentiful, the lake so glassy and life so good, the merganser turned sideways, showing me his back and flanks shining with diamond droplets of water. His white breast feathers caught the light in a way I have seen only a few times before in my life, reflecting a peach glow as though lit from within, as though carved from alabaster.

In 1972, upon the 50th anniversary of the discovery of King Tut's tomb, the Egyptian government sent 50 artifacts to London to be displayed by the British Museum. As a first-year graduate student in Egyptology, I went there to see the exhibit, never dreaming I would be privileged a few years later to be in Egypt.

Along with thousands of other tourists, I waited four hours in line. Inside the museum, guards were posted every few feet to keep the objects safe. "Move along, move along," they intoned whenever anyone stopped for more than a few seconds to look. I shuffled along with the crowd, gazing at jewelry, furniture, weapons, and funerary items created more than 33 centuries ago.

But when I came to object Number 7, an alabaster chalice, I stopped in my tracks, transfixed. The cup was only seven inches high, carved in the shape of a white lotus blossom, flanked by clusters of un-

Male Common Merganser ©Gregg Thompson

opened lily buds for handles. Seated atop each lily cluster on either side was the figure of Heh, god of eternity, kneeling upon a bowl, the hieroglyphic sign for universality. Heh was holding emblems symbolizing life and long years. Inscribed in blue around the cup's edge was a wish for the king. As the crowd backed up behind me, I tried to translate.

A guard came to see what was holding up the flow of traffic. "Move along," he started to say. But then he saw I was copying the hieroglyphics into my notebook. He must have realized I was a student, because he told me to sit down beside the plinth holding the chalice. "You'll be able to write better like that," he said kindly. "Take your time." Everyone in the crowd smiled their agreement.

I still have that notebook, and the wish for the king I translated: "May your soul live and you spend millions of years, you who love Thebes, sitting with your face to the north wind and your eyes beholding happiness."

My eyes beheld perfect happiness on that day, as warmly glowing in my memory as the alabaster of the cup that radiated a soft peach

Female Common Merganser © Tim Kuhn

color, like luminous embers of life heated from within. Alabaster has the property of letting light enter a few millimeters before it is reflected back out again, making the stone seem warm and alive. When carved thinly, alabaster becomes translucent, adding delicate shades of pink and gold to its palette, the exact same color as the merganser's breast I observed all these many years and miles later.

"I remember," I whispered to the still-smiling merganser before he turned away and the glow dimmed. Not gone, though. Never gone, because alive in memory.

"Speak my name and I live again," the king commanded his followers. And so I did: Horus, Mighty Bull, perfect in birth, goodly of laws, who makes peaceful the Two Lands of Egypt, Horus of Gold, exalted of crowns, who pleases the gods, king of Upper and Lower Egypt, lord of the Two Lands, lord of all the forms of Re the Sun, Tutankhamun, given life forever."

Speak the name, and evoke the memories. Let your loved ones live forever in your heart. Pass the memories to the next generation, and the next, so that a part of us will live and be loved for all time.

The merganser paddled out of sight beyond East Point, and I returned to reality. But which reality? Did the merganser represent the goofiness I had displayed earlier when I had sounded my submarine klaxon horn and amused an onlooker, or did it instead symbolize the sublime oneness of spirit I had experienced when I remembered a long-lost king, and with him, my long-ago loved ones?

The ancient Egyptians would not have been troubled by this dichotomy. They had the ability to live with contradiction and were perfectly at ease with duality. Many things for them came in twos. They lived on the Two Banks of the Nile, the East Bank for the living and the West Bank for the dead. Their kings ruled the Two Lands of ancient Egypt, the Black Land of the farms and the Red Land of the desert. Their universe consisted of this world and the netherworld. "Why choose one reality?" the ancients might ask. "Why not both?"

For when life makes us laugh at its silliness and glow with its transcendence, aren't both a form of joy?

7. Let This Be a Lesson

Although the head of a Pine Siskin is approximately one-2,500th the size of a human's, we could learn a thing or two from this little bird brain. Pine Siskins are diminutive members of the finch family who gather together in large numbers in winter to range all over our region, searching for one of their favorite foods, alder cone seeds.

Pine Siskins are uncommon at the Fill, probably because there aren't enough alder trees to attract a flock for long. Luckily, though, this year's cone crop has been unusually abundant, and we have been hosting three large flocks for at least a week. I estimate there are more than 600 siskins altogether. When the birds change trees, the sky darkens as their bodies pelt through the air.

The presence of so many Pine Siskins has given me a rare chance to study these birds up close and personal, especially when they settle down for a rest after feeding in the early morning. Their favorite rest stop is Boy Scout Pond, where the siskins perch in the tops of the tall cottonwood trees. There, they exchange views, do a little preening, take a nap—whatever appeals. I guess they figure they have so many eyes looking out for predators, it's safe to relax.

Not all the siskins are content to laze about on just one perch, though. Several seem to be a little twitchy, like guards who think an enemy is about to spring from ambush. They could be right. A Cooper's Hawk has been lurking in the marsh nearby and might enjoy a siskin snack.

Rather than flee the scene, though, the twitchy siskins simply fly from their home flock in one tree to join a neighboring flock in

Pine Siskin © Doug Parrott

another tree. Nobody in the second flock tries to drive away the newbies. On the contrary, guests are welcomed with a few nods and chitterings, then the whole flock goes back to preening or napping.

The ease with which siskins change allegiance, as it were, has made me envious. We humans value communal living at least as much as the siskins do, but human loyalty to our own group is much more absolute than it is for the birds. For us, the entry ticket to get into a group seems to be punched with an exclusivity clause. Once we join one group, everyone else becomes an outsider, usually alien, often enemy. Us against them.

Sometimes our human rivalry is good-humored, as when our former governor, Christine Gregoire, bet against the governor of Wisconsin on a Seattle Seahawks-Green Bay Packers football game. Gregoire wagered Cougar Gold cheese (famously made at Washington State University) against Governor Jim Doyle's stake of Midwest bratwurst. Wisconsin football fans, you may recall, are notorious for wearing cheese-wedge hats, I suppose because the state has a lot of cows and makes large amounts of cheese, so why not put some cheddar on your head?

Gregoire answered this question with wry humor, throwing down the cheese gauntlet, so to speak. "It may seem odd to bet cheese against the cheeseheads," she said, "but we think Governor Doyle would be impressed by the quality of Cougar Gold....The cheese from Washington is so good we wouldn't want to waste it by putting it on our heads."

Of course, many times our human rivalries are not at all good humored. War, genocide, terrorism, prejudice, oppression—all are related, in large measure, to our propensity to exclude and demonize those unlike ourselves.

This strategy might have worked well when our ancestors were hunters and gatherers and food supplies were iffy. In those times, people might welcome a lone stranger into the tribe if they needed an additional spouse or a skilled hunter. But a whole band of strangers? Strangers were potential rivals for limited resources. Better kill them or drive them away.

Nowadays, though, most of the food we eat appears in a supermarket, not in the wild, and it comes from all over the world. So do our clothes, our cars, even our ideas. "To state the obvious," said IBM's former CEO Sam Palmisano at a THINK Conference for future leaders held in New York in 2011, "we've never been more interconnected. Economically, socially, technologically, our world has become one big system of systems. That's different than being an assemblage of markets or nations or industries. We have global systems of transportation, energy, communications, food and water, commerce, security, and even more."

Palmisano acknowledged the many problems an interconnected world faces: the volatility of markets, systems failures in banking and resource distribution, persistent unemployment, unmet expectations, and violence. But he also pointed out that never before have we been so well equipped to solve any problem, no matter how big.

Cooper's Hawk © Doug Parrott

For one thing, we have access to enormous sources of information. "There are upwards of a trillion interconnected and intelligent objects and organisms, all on the internet," he said. "All of this is generating vast stores of information. It's estimated that there will be 44 times as much data over the next decade than we have today, reaching 35 zetabytes by 2020. For those of you who aren't of a math orientation, like myself, a zetabyte is one followed by 21 zeroes.

"Thanks to computation analytics, we can make sense of this data in something like real time. This enables very different kinds of insight and foresight in decision-making. It actually provides the opportunity to address many of the systemic issues that the world is frustrated by today."

A second resource is people—people connected to each other over great distances in real time, people who thus have the capability to collaborate on a vast scale. "The most active and successful leaders today see themselves as part of a global community," Palmisano said. "They are hungry to learn from other people....What I find most encouraging is that forward-thinking leaders...are innovating in ways that create virtuous circles for a generation or more. They're not gaming the system. They're building systems."

Pine Siskins can't build anything larger than a nest. We can. The question is, how can we continue to do so in a globally connected world when our antiquated instincts tell us that our differences must equate to animosities, that rivals are enemies?

Mourning Cloak butterfly © Idie Ulsh

On my camp stool, watching the siskins preen and chatter with each other, a movement in the grass caught my eye. An overwintering Mourning Cloak butterfly was opening its wings to the light. It perched on a grass stem that was totally encased in hoarfrost. I looked out over the field and saw that every blade of grass was similarly wrapped in white crystals. While I watched, the weak Sun of winter rose over the eastern ridge and lightly caressed the tops of the grass. Even in its enfeebled state, the sunlight was strong enough to melt the ice. The butterfly and the field grew warmer, and water droplets began to form on the tips of each grass stem. The diamond drops trembled in the almost imperceptible breeze, then fell, forming tiny pools on the ground.

The transformation of ice into water made me realize there are different ways to join together. One way is to unite completely, leaving behind all our differences, losing ourselves like a drop of water joining a pool. Another way is to add ourselves and our differences to a group, enhancing it like an ice crystal extending feathery new rays.

Perhaps we humans will never be able to give up our need to belong to an exclusive group, to be one part of a unique, larger identity. Perhaps we will always cling to our own culture, our own ethnicity. And maybe that's a good thing. Diversity is a strength of our species because it enables us to explore—all at once—innumerable solutions to the big problems we face. If we have infinite challenges, we also have infinite creativity.

Then let us keep our differences alive, but let us also value those differences. Let us share each other's knowledge and resources so all of us may improve our lives. If we can do that, our differences will become the wellspring of our humanity rather than our downfall.

Alice Houston, deputy superintendent of Seattle Public Schools and a committed advocate for equality, once told me, "We will overcome racial prejudice and the evils of disparity when we can look into the face of every child, no matter the race, and say, 'This one is my child, too.'"[1]

8. Vistas

Vistas in the city can be very hard to come by. "As far as the eye can see" usually means you get to gaze out over a block or two of buildings, and that's it.

When I feel the need for a more expansive vista, I take myself to Montlake Fill, where the views are wide and wonderful. One of my favorite spots stretches north from Wahkiakum Lane over the rolling hills of Paulson Prairie. Paulson Prairie is bordered on the north by the Youth Farm and the graceful cottonwoods of Corporation Yard Pond. In summer, it is dotted with spikes of camas that bloom palely white or deep purple, adding droplets of living color to the backdrop of drab, brown grass. In winter, the fields turn green, watered by the rainfall that blesses Seattle so abundantly. The contrast of green fields and gray skies is beautiful.

To get the full benefit of the view, I nearly always set up my camp stool on the green verge of Wahkiakum Lane just east of the North Blue Forest. There, I can rest my eyes on the serenity of this prairie paradise. Mind you, serene does not necessarily mean quiet. Coyotes sometimes wander through here, on the lookout for the rodents that are attracted by the grass seeds, fruit, and insects that characterize this habitat. Birds are fond of these attractions, too, and forage here in large numbers.

Such was the case one winter day last week. The prairie was alive with birds. A platoon of finches was dining on the dried hawthorne fruit that still festooned the December trees. Their noisy enjoyment attracted a flock of American Robins, who began tearing off berries

Eastern Phoebe at the Fill on December 8, 2012 © Ryan Merrill

like greedy two-year-olds afraid that someone else would eat the goodies first. Suddenly, a flash of olive-gray wings drew my eye, and a strange bird landed on the remnants of the giant nest the art students have built in the field. (As an aside, I've been asked by many nonbirders over the years what kind of bird would build a nest the size of a Volkswagen, and believe me, it's been hard to restrain myself from making up answers.)

The strange bird stood for a moment on the artwork, swiveled its tail to sketch an infinity symbol in the invisible air, gave a musical chirp, and then flitted to a bramble growing beside the Blue Forest. There it paused for a long moment, eyeing me while it chirped, then it flicked open its wings and was gone.

"Holy cow!" I exclaimed, leaping to my feet. My camp stool shot backwards like an expended booster rocket. Birds burst out of bushes in flocks I hadn't known were there, and all the robins fled to the tops of the cottonwoods, where they straightened their feathers and glared. "What the heck was that?" I asked them, not that robins ever answer such questions.

I began to tally the field marks: flycatcher family, based on shape and behavior; very plain upper parts; whitish belly washed with pale yellow; no wing bars, no eye ring. One by one, I eliminated all the flycatchers ever seen in North America, until I was left with just one: Eastern Phoebe. It seemed preposterous. Eastern Phoebes are drab birds of the eastern United States. They like to live in Kansas during the summer, unlike anyone else I know. When fall approaches, they migrate south to Texas, Mexico, or Florida. What was one doing in Washington in December??

I foraged in the tall grass until I found my camp stool, then hurried back home to post this rarity on Tweeters, the birders' online forum. Within seconds, the word went out: Rare Eastern Phoebe at Montlake Fill. Birders began to arrive from all points in the Seattle area. Of course by then, the bird had disappeared. But luckily, my birder friend John Puschock relocated the little guy and started taking photos. It was confirmed: I had added a new species to the bird records of the Fill, records that date back to 1895.

I felt myself grinning ear to ear. I had a new bird to add to my life list of birds at the Fill, where I've seen a grand total of 204 species. For me, part of the joy of birding is keeping lists of all the birds I see. I have a list of all the North American birds I've found; a yard list of all the birds who have shown up or flown over my yard; and of course, my Fill list. Every January 1, I start a new list of Fill birds for the year. My best year was 2009, when I saw 159 different species. This year got off to a great start: It's getting near the end of June, and I've already seen 138 species, including two new species never at the Fill before: Black-billed Magpie and Alder Flycatcher. Naturally, I keep a separate list of all the newbies.

Bird lists are not the only lists I like. Whenever I travel, I make a list of what I need to bring. Before I go to the supermarket, I make a list of what I need to buy. On Sunday, I list the dinner menu for the week. In December, I send out greeting cards to all my friends and family—I know precisely how many cards I've sent because I keep a list. One of my most important lists is my list of things to do. Actually, I have two To Do lists. One I make weekly; the second is a daily list. I love crossing things off my To Do lists, but in all the years I've kept them, I have never crossed off every item on the lists. Some days, I'm lucky if I cross off only one or two.

You might think this would bother me. After all, the purpose of a list is to organize your life so it becomes manageable, efficient, stress-free. Making lists of the things you have to do allows you to allot enough time during the day to complete your obligations and thus free yourself to do, with a clear conscience, the things you love. Lists give you control over the chaos of modern life.

So why can I never manage to do everything on my list? Are my obligations so numerous, my drudgeries so onerous that it is impossible to get through them all? And if they are, why doesn't this freak me out? For the answer, I turn to Japanese artist Hokusai. According to art historian Louis Frédéric Nussbaum in his book, *Japan Encyclopedia*, when Hokusai reached age 73, he wrote:

"From around the age of six, I had the habit of sketching from life. I became an artist, and from 50 on began producing works that won some reputation. But nothing I did before the age of 70 was worthy of attention. At 73, I began to grasp the structures of birds and beasts, insects and fish, and of the way plants grow. If I go on trying, I will surely understand them still better by the time I am 86, so that by 90 I will have penetrated to their essential nature. At 100, I may well have a positively divine understanding of them, while at 130, 140, or more I will have reached the stage where every dot and every stroke I paint will be alive. May Heaven, that grants long life, give me the chance to prove this is no lie."

"If I go on trying." Isn't that a marvelous phrase? It means there is no limit to the heights you can reach or the achievements you can make. So you—and all that your life embodies—can always keep growing. It also means that trying is the most hopeful thing you can do in life. Trying may not guarantee success, but it does guarantee the *chance* of success. As Penny Tweedy, the owner of the great racehorse Secretariat, once said, "You never know how far you can run unless you run."

Over the years, I have tried to understand why it is I am so thrilled when I see a new bird species at the Fill. Part of the answer is that watching my Fill life list grow a little longer each year validates the fact that the Earth is still filled with great diversity, and that wildlife, however threatened by human activity, is resilient. I am glad to witness this whenever I can. It's a counterbalance to the gloomier messages about endangered species that might otherwise be hopelessly overwhelming.

However true that answer, it is not the whole story. Hokusai made me realize I never want to reach the end of my list of things to do. I never want to complete all the obligations I have in life. Heck, I don't even want to eat every item on my weekly menu—how dull to be confined to a diet set in stone, even if I am the one doing the setting. Most important to me as a birder, I never want to complete my list of all the birds to ever come to the Fill. I hope every year brings more new species for me to record and share with everyone.

For that is my last and best list of all: Birds I have yet to see at the Fill. White-faced Ibises are on that list. They are the North American version of Egypt's Sacred Ibis, which to the ancients was the god of writing and wisdom.

I think about how profound it was for the ancient Egyptians to combine writing and wisdom into one devotional entity. Writing requires us to become wise, or at least to get organized in our thinking. But more than that, writing enables us to pass our knowledge to future generations, and so all humankind benefits. To me, the ibis is a metaphorical, almost mythical bird, scarcely real and yet still hoped for, hoped for because its beauty will help me understand the essentials of wild nature and encourage me to give to others whatever insights I have gained.

Joseph Campbell, the famous mythologist, calls understanding myth "going behind the mask." I cannot leave this life until I go behind the mask, until I discover the key to unlock the mysterious intersection where wild nature meets the human spirit, until I tell all the stories within me, until I understand my own art of writing as deeply as Hokusai wanted to understand his, until every word I write will be alive.

Until I see ibises.

Coyote at Montlake Fill ©Kathrine Lloyd

Part II
Spring

9. Behold, Thou Art Fair

The Great Blue Herons are starting to gather at the Fill again. They've been scarce and hard to find for the past couple of months, but as spring approaches, so do they. Their favorite place to congregate is the top of Dempsey Gym on the southwest corner of the Fill.

In the mornings—not too early!—the herons slowly and majestically float in from the west like avian zeppelins. When they reach the gym, they extend their preposterously long landing gear and alight on top of the curved roof. There, they hunch themselves into living statues and do what? Commune with the great unknown? Exchange telepathic thoughts? See who can be the best heron by playing freeze tag the longest?

I have no idea. To my eye, they stand on the roof doing absolutely nothing for hours. Then some of them condescend to fish in the sloughs and ponds of the Fill, while others float slowly—and majestically!—back where they came from.

The herons do this every spring prior to their major annual effort: the Heron Big Sit. Big Sits, I should mention, are a tactic we birders use to raise money for charity. Big Sitters go around to all our friends and relatives and twist their arms until they agree to donate a certain amount of money for every species seen by the sitters while we are planted in one place for one day, from sunrise to sunset.

Herons are even better at sitting in one place than humans are, only in their case, they don't raise money; they raise chicks. They do so in communal nesting areas called rookeries. The herons of the Fill have established a rookery on the UW campus near Drumheller

Fountain. The rookery began with just a couple of nests about five years ago. Last year, there were more than 30 active nests. This year looks even better. I counted 53 Great Blue Herons on top of the gym yesterday, and there were almost as many among the cattails bordering the shore. The slough between Canoe Island and the mainland hosted one heron every five feet.

Great Blue Herons often look to me like they each just stuck a toe in an electric socket—foom!—and their feathers jut out in shock. Other times, they remind me of Emperor Joseph II's criticism of one of Mozart's new operas, in the film *Amadeus*. The emperor thought Mozart's composition was too long. He suggested Mozart shorten it by deleting a few notes. To paraphrase: "There are too many feathers. Simply cut a few and it will be perfect."

But just as Mozart was completely unable to cut a note without ruining the perfection of his opera, a heron needs every one of its feathers, too. Some it needs to keep warm; others to stay dry. Some it hopes will attract a mate; others are used to intimidate a rival. Feathers can signal danger, announce an imminent attack, or hide the wearer from predators. Of course, the preeminent use of feathers is to fly, whether it be to provide lift, help steer, or smooth out the bird's contours to improve air flow. All these feathers are piled onto the bird—in rows, stacks, heaps, and single plumes. There are so many you can scarcely hope to count them all.

The feathers take a lot of care. They must be oiled and smoothed, fluffed up and patted down. Sometimes the feathers itch, and the heron must raise one foot in a careful balancing act to scratch the offending area. Eventually the feathers wear out, and then the bird must molt.

All birds molt their feathers, usually once a year, but each does it on its own schedule. Some birds molt just before they head south on their long flight to their winter territory. Some wait until they're home for the winter. Others molt soon after the fledglings leave the nest, when the parents have time to draw a breath.

Herons never seem to molt. On the contrary, they always seem to carry an overabundance of supply. Logically, you know they must lose a feather here and there. But like all the best performers, they never let you see them drop a note.

I am grateful to the Great Blue Herons of the Fill because they make me look good. Whenever nonbirding friends or family members show up, wanting me to guide them on a walk around the Fill, I pray that a Great Blue will be somewhere on the site. New birders, I have found, are not impressed by the little brown jobs that I love to watch so much—the shorebirds, sparrows, and finches that enliven my favorite place on Earth. No, newbies want to see something big

Great Blue Heron hiding behind its wing © Doug Parrott

Great Blue Heron stabbing a fish © Doug Parrott

and flashy. They want action, preferably lethal—the avian equivalent of a Hollywood film's exploding helicopter.

Great Blue Herons deliver. They're big. They're showy. And they stab their prey. Fish, frogs, rodents, snakes—Great Blues are not fussy stabbers, so the chance of seeing them in action is always high. Take the heron who often hunts on Southwest Pond, for example. He can be found stalking the shallows almost any time, his mad yellow eyes fixed on the water, his neck spring-loaded, his saber-beak poised.

One day, two friends from Maryland, Gosia and Bob, asked me to take them to the Fill. Gosia and Bob are seasoned travelers who seek adventure all over the world. They are as open-minded as two people can be, but they are not birders. So when they started down the Loop Trail with me in the lead, I prayed for my favorite heron, Old Reliable, to be in position.

Luckily, he was. Just as we came up to Southwest Pond, he glided out of the lily pads, sliding one long leg forward, then the other. When he froze into a statue en garde, so did we. We all held our breath. Then—pow!—the heron's beak rocketed out, stabbed the water with a mighty splash, and came back with a wriggling sunfish. Casually, the heron flipped the fish off his bill, caught it headfirst, and gulped. I couldn't think how a disk-shaped fish the size of a dinner plate would fit into a tube-shaped throat less than half its diameter. Nevertheless, when the heron gave a few more gulps, the sunfish disappeared down the hatch.

Gosia and Bob were entranced. "Oh, oh," they said, unable to find fitting words to describe the experience.

We walked on a while in silence, sharing the transcendent emotion the heron had engendered. As we approached a bend in the trail, I stopped and made a sweeping motion with my arm, encompassing this place that is my spiritual home, this Eden on Earth. "I have lost all perspective about the beauty of the Fill," I said. "I cannot look at it anymore with objectivity. I see too many moments in my mind's eye like the one we just had. But I am curious. How does a person with no previous experience judge the beauty of this place? You've never come here before. How does it strike you?"

Gosia looked out at the brown prairie that lay before us, dotted with random tufts of greening grass, the leafless willows around Main Pond just beginning to bud, the tall cottonwoods of Yesler Swamp in the distance, reaching for the sky with their still bare, woody fingers. "Well," she said, "it is pretty scraggly."

All righty. So now I know. The Fill is scraggly.

Since that day, I have often walked the Loop Trail, trying to see the inherent, omnipresent, timeless scraggliness of the Fill. It seems important, somehow, to keep this in mind, a matter of telling the truth to myself. But I just can't do it. I have gone too deeply into the heart of beauty itself.

Beauty, you see, is not just a pleasant collection of line, form, color, or symmetry. Beauty starts out that way, yes. But the more we come to love something that looks beautiful, the more we can embrace the essence of its beauty. As love and beauty become inextricably intertwined, the importance of outward appearance fades away into the blurry image of past remembrance, as does everything we experienced when we were young. For as the wisdom of age grows, we learn that beauty loved becomes beauty felt, not just seen. And such beauty, true beauty, can never fade. It only grows richer with each passing year.

Bullfrog © Doug Parrott

10. Forever Young

March has been chill and gray this year, a reminder that winter still has us firmly in its withered grip. But not for long. The Earth is slowly but surely tilting us back toward the life-giving Sun. Spring is on the way.

The birds know this. Although it's still early in the year, our resident birds are already getting a jump on nesting season. Mallards are pairing up. American Robins are singing their chirpiest songs. Red-winged Blackbird males are showing off their red epaulets to each other and seeing who can swell up to make the loudest bagpipe.

Meanwhile, the birds who migrated here last fall to spend the winter with us are getting ready to head north to their breeding grounds in the bogs, tundra, or taiga, where the insects are plentiful and the living is easy. Sparrows and warblers, wrens, kinglets, and waterfowl are all becoming visibly restless and eager to leave, like college kids yearning for spring break. They know they still have work to do down here, fattening up for the trip, but their minds are on the adventure ahead, not the drudgery on hand.

Ruby-crowned Kinglets are especially impatient, flitting nervously from bush to bush as they forage for insects, eggs, and larvae too small for me to see, even with my binoculars. Of course, kinglets are always impatient, never still for more than an instant. But at this time of year, they are as quick to fight as they are to flit. That's why they're called kinglets: Supposedly, they all think they deserve to be king of the hill, and they don't care who knows it.

Usually, they establish dominance by parting the olive-green feathers on the tops of their heads and raising the tiny, fire-red plumes that lie underneath. Then they shine their heads at each other. But in early spring, they go farther than mere head-shining. They actually go after each other, chasing one another around and around a bush or a tree limb, trying to give a rival a memorable peck on the behind. Not that they're serious about defending a territory or impressing a mate. All that lies north in the future. I guess the fighting we see down here is mere sparring for practice.

One kinglet has been particularly feisty this season. He's set up temporary housekeeping on a rosebush in the South Blue Forest. Here he takes on all comers. Sometimes his challengers are other kinglets looking for a fight. But his greatest rival is an Anna's Hummingbird with big ideas, who has laid claim to the entire area west of the forest.

When these two meet, there is no quarter given. The fighting is fast and furious, accompanied by plenty of tiny yelling and name-calling. Usually, it is the kinglet who loses. He is slower than his rival and has a much smaller beak. But that doesn't stop him from coming back for more. Like the crime boss Fergie Colm in Ben Affleck's movie, *The Town,* the kinglet believes in never staying down for long. "Still in the ring. Still taking punches. Still ahead on points."

Spring is the time of rebirth, when new life returns to the north and all becomes green again. The young joggers who trot around the Loop Trail throw off their sweatpants and heavy coats and don short sleeves and even skimpier shorts. Youth claims the spring for its own, breezing past the aged as though we were standing still. We almost are. One young runner passed me while I was doddering near the Reading Rocks the other day. She disappeared around the bend going full speed and soon came back around again, barely puffing. Meanwhile I had advanced to the curly willow tree, approximately ten paces further down the trail. In my defense, I was birding, as always, so I cannot be expected to move at the speed of light. Still, I must have seemed to that young woman as though I were positively statuesque in my immobility. Mummified.

Anna's Hummingbird stretching © Tim Kuhn

Forever Young

She gave me a quick, pitying glance. I knew what she was thinking. It was something along the lines of, "Gosh, I hope I never get that old!" I thought the same thing in my youth. Seeing elders with their walkers taking eons to cross the street against the light, holding up the line while they sorted through the change in their purses as they tried to pay for their groceries, puttering along at 20 mph in the fast lane—I was often impatient with the slowness of age, with its befuddlement and lack of energy. When I wasn't rolling my eyes at how out of it the elderly seemed, I was smiling indulgently because of how cute they were. Old age seemed almost comical to me. I chuckled when centenarian George Burns said, "At my age, I don't even buy green bananas."

I never thought I'd be the little old lady clutching the steering wheel of my elderly sedan, my eyes barely reaching above the point

Ruby-crowned Kinglet © Gregg Thompson

where the windshield meets the dashboard, my turn signal continuously blinking because I've forgotten to shut it off, but what the heck, I'll be turning it on again sometime soon, so no matter.

I'm not that little old lady yet, but I can see the time coming when I will be. In fact, I aspire to that time, because what is the alternative? As comedian Bill Cosby says, "I'm old, not dead." Of course, he is also famous for saying, "Old is always fifteen years from now."

As I approach the time when I can't put old off for another fifteen years, I have discovered that aging gracefully takes courage. The effort of getting up and getting dressed is real effort. The decision to go for a walk calls for commitment. Reading a book requires special equipment—reading glasses numbered 1, 2, 3, or 4, depending on how far away you hold your book before you don the glasses—and you have to keep buying new pairs because you frequently step on the old ones that fell off your face while you were "only resting your eyes for a minute."

But age has its joys too. There is the happiness of knowing who I am, and why I am here. There is the peace that comes from laying down old baggage, the baggage I never should have hauled around for as long as I did, but thank goodness, I'm not hauling it another step now. Age grants perspective, allowing us to see that obstacles which blocked us so completely in the past have been transformed into valuable experience that enriches us now. Pain that seemed unbearable in our younger days has faded enough to become bearable because we have grown in strength. Age gives us permission to take life slowly and thus see the glorious minutiae of a little kinglet fighting an even littler hummingbird.

I love those little guys because they show me what it takes to stay engaged in life, to feel the renaissance of spring no matter your birth date. Like them, I too am still in the ring. Still taking punches. Still ahead on points.

11. A Bit of a Fwap

I think I have finally figured out how the Double-crested Cormorants hang onto the light standards around the baseball diamond on the western border of the Fill. These light standards are mounted on tall poles. They consist of struts that stick out straight on either side of the center pole. Mounted on the struts are several lamps, covered by shiny, curved reflectors. The cormorants love to perch on the light standards and do so by the dozen.

It's easy to see how they manage to hold onto their preferred perches, namely, the horizontal struts on either side of the center pole. The cormorants merely wrap their webbed feet around the struts and grip hard. This gives them a secure hold. Even when the wind blows, as it was doing ferociously one day this spring, the cormorants can hang on, although I think their knuckles were turning white from the strain (assuming cormorants have knuckles). The birds swayed back and forth with each gust, like jacks-in-a-box bobbing on springs, but they did not get blown off.

What's a lot harder to figure out is how the cormorants who perch on the curved lamps hold on. The reflectors are highly polished half-spheres with a surface that looks as slippery as ice in a hockey rink. Yet the cormorants who stand on them stick so well they scarcely wave in the breeze. If their feathers weren't being blown all catawampus by the wind, you'd think the birds were statues mounted onto the lamps with rebar.

My own theory centers around the morphological control that I postulate cormorants must exercise over their feet. Normally, cormorants' feet are flat as pancakes. According to my theory, though,

Double-crested Cormorants gripping a light stand with their feet © Doug Parrott

if they wish, they can curve their feet into convex cups. When they press their now-hemispherical feet down onto the lamps, the feet stick like suction cups.

Yesterday, I was close enough to the light standards to test my theory. A cormorant came flying in from the lake, stretched out its legs and landed on a lamp. I strained my ears to the maximum, and I distinctly heard a thup! sound as it landed. I listened even harder as the bird changed its position. Again, I heard the thup! thup! thup! of the cups getting stuck and unstuck when the bird shifted position. I was right! Cormorants *can* turn their feet into octopus-like suckers. In fact, I imagine with suction cups like that, they could walk up the sides of buildings if they wanted to.

Now, the official Washington Bird Records Committee (WBRC) might argue that my field observation is no real proof that cormorants have suction-cup feet. After all, I was the only observer, and I did not record the sound. Who is to say whether what I heard was really a thup? Possibly it was a fwap, which would be a strong indication that the bird's feet remained flat. Or maybe what I heard was just an ordinary whap, which could be the result of an indeterminate collision of bird foot on light standard.

In cases like this—when something new to science is reported by only one observer without any technical backup—the records committee tries to assess the expertise of the reporter. "Is Connie qualified to tell a thup from a fwap or a whap?" they might ask.

It's a tough question. For one thing, I freely admit that I am not the greatest at identifying birds by ear. Unlike the best birders—who can hear a mere chirp and immediately determine whether the chirper is, say, a Lincoln's Sparrow, a Yellow-rumped Warbler, or a Ruby-crowned Kinglet—I sometimes struggle to identify the most commonplace songs. If I am poor at identifying bird song, wouldn't it follow that I would also be poor at identifying bird footfalls?

Somehow, if I ever decide to submit my report, the records committee will have to come up with an answer to this difficult question. It isn't simple, and I do not envy them the task. The WBRC is a group of serious citizen-scientists who assess birders' reports of rare sightings. They perform a crucial yet thankless service, affirming or

Double-crested Cormorant with feet flat as pancakes © Gregg Thompson

denying the identification of rare birds. I say "thankless" because birders who make such reports often care deeply about personally accompanying our sightings into the record books. In short, we want credit. If the committee denies a sighting, some of us get steamed. If the committee approves a sighting but gives the wrong person credit, or if the committee spreads the credit around too broadly, we can blow a gasket.

Yet, despite our readiness to take offense, all of us birders acknowledge the importance of the committee's work. Keeping track of the birds in our state helps us make good decisions about habitat preservation. For example, thanks in part to citizen-scientists, King County's Quartermaster Harbor, located between Vashon and Maury Islands, was declared an Important Bird Area (IBA). IBAs are internationally identified wildlife areas that are the focus of special conservation concern and effort. Washington State has 74 such IBAs. Without the help of volunteer birders, it is doubtful we would be able to justify the nomination of any such sites.

Because their work is so vital, the records committee usually prefers to err on the side of caution. Hence the sometimes heated disagreements. That's partly why I have yet to submit my report on cormorants' feet. I'm not sure I want to stir up the contention that would be bound to follow my submission. As I grow older, I find myself picking my battles judiciously, although I would hate to think that age has brought me to the safe harbor where I never rock the boat. On the contrary, I like to think that in old age, I will be one of those feisty seniors who carries an umbrella so she can whap uppity whippersnappers on the backs of their legs when they displease her. Or fwap them, if I'm feeling weak and decrepit.

I did ask a couple of birder friends to come out to the baseball diamond and listen with me one day a few weeks ago. We gathered on Canal Road between the Lagoon and the baseball stadium and looked up. Sure enough, one light standard was loaded with cormorants. Unfortunately, the cormorants were all asleep. We decided to wait for a new cormorant to show up and push one of the other ones off. While we waited, hoping our subject would soon appear, we passed the time as birders typically do on such watches: We talked about rare birds we had experienced in the past.

Suddenly, a Double-crested Cormorant came flapping ponderously up from the Lagoon. As it neared its desired perch, it began to croak hoarsely, alerting the other cormorants that an interloper was about to crash their slumber party. Everyone began croaking, including a few of us birders. That's probably why, when the newcomer finally hit the light, the sound was somewhat indistinct. There was too much interference. The cormorants settled down again and went back to sleep. We were left deep in thought.

"I think what I heard was a fwap," said one friend tentatively. No one likes to deprive a hopeful record-finder of a new find, and she didn't want to go against my report of a thup. But truth is truth. "The sibilance of the initial consonant was breathier and longer than the 'th' of a typical thup. Fffffwwwap," she demonstrated, spraying us liberally with saliva.

More silence. Then, said another, "Yes, but did you notice the lack of staccato in the vowel? The 'a' in a fwap is staccato—fwap!—and this sound was drawn out, more of an 'uuuhhhh' than a quick 'a.' I think the vowel sound is diagnostic. Clearly a thuuuuuhp."

The most dyspeptic birder in the group chimed in. "I don't understand how you can definitively identify the sound as either a fwap or a thup. There was too much background noise. I think we're going to have to settle for a simple, generic whap."

Nobody was happy with this suggestion. We birders like specificity. Generic IDs seem so wimpy. But there you have it. We were obviously in three irreconcilable camps: the whappers, the fwappers, and the thups. Without substantial agreement among my friends, I don't see how I can go to the records committee.

Thus, the mystery of exactly how a cormorant can stick onto a slippery surface has yet to be solved. I have great hope that someday, a young ornithologist will accept the challenge of resolving this issue. Until then, it must remain one of the many unknowns that will keep us birders coming back into the field for as long as there are birds to learn about, and birders who care.

12. Étude in Gray Minor

The photographers have been complaining about the dim light that has plagued our spring this year. "It's not like I can bring a flash out here and get any kind of reasonable exposure," one grumbled, carefully bundling his 500 mm f/4 lens and camera body into the back of his SUV.

I know what he means. Gray skies are one thing, a phenomenon to be expected and even welcomed in Seattle. But gray for us is usually silvery light, tinged with just enough sunshine to lightly burnish each tree, each blade of grass, with unearthly beauty. Or our gray might be pewter, a darker, less shiny light that softens every surface it caresses. My favorite gray is stormy, with blue-black clouds that make the yellow-green poplar catkins glow like candlesticks when lit by the occasional match of sunlight that sneaks through.

But this spring, our gray skies have been none of these. The low clouds have been so thick they have robbed the world of all hue, turning everything into a washed-out monochrome that lets us discern only form and line. It has been nearly impossible to resolve enough colors to be able to distinguish bird from branch, let alone bird from bird. On these grayest of days, it can be very easy to just stay home and be glad we live in the Age of Electricity, when we can bring as much light inside as we wish. Birding in absentia seems more fun than slogging around in the cold of reality.

But, as my husband frequently tells me, "Those birds won't watch themselves." That's his way of encouraging me to respect my art. He knows I need to be out in nature every day, both to achieve peace of mind and to inspire creativity.

Étude in Gray Minor

Sora © Tim Kuhn

Then he laid another quote on me. John maintains a gigantic database of quotes, which he trots out whenever he wants to make a point that he thinks has been better made by someone more famous. In this case, he chose Ansel Adams: "Our lives at times seem a study in contrast…love and hate, birth and death, right and wrong…everything seen in absolutes of black and white. Too often we are not aware that it is the shades of gray that add depth and meaning to the starkness of those extremes."

John looked up hopefully from his computer and beamed more encouragement my way. Birds and philosophy, his look said, what more did I need to get my pump primed?

While I always appreciate John's chirpy support, I have to admit his help might go down better if he weren't stretched out on the couch, drinking coffee and letting the heater blow warm air over him. Luckily on this day, John got some unexpected support from the *New York Times,* which ran a terrific interview of Stephen Hawking. Dr. Hawking is a famous physicist and cosmologist who is almost completely disabled by his progressive disease, amyotrophic lateral sclerosis (ALS). All he can control anymore is a cheek muscle. Using this one muscle, he painfully twitches messages onto his computer, which translates his words into mechanical speech. The interview was mostly conducted in writing, for obvious reasons, and took days.

One of the questions was: "Given all you've experienced, what words would you offer someone who has been diagnosed with a serious illness, perhaps ALS?"

Hawking answered: "My advice to other disabled people would be, concentrate on things your disability doesn't prevent you doing well, and don't regret the things it interferes with. Don't be disabled in spirit, as well as physically."

I realized I have missed the spring spirit this year, that exhilaration when joy bubbles up as the Sun rises, birds start to sing, and the river of migrating birds that flows northward this time of year could carry *anything* here. I have missed the can't-wait feeling of anticipation that each new arrival brings from the south, the affirmation of life ongoing, of nature resilient, of a spiritual force greater and more long-lasting than ourselves. I have let myself become disabled in spirit. I needed a kick in the pants, and Dr. Hawking supplied it.

With his words echoing in my mind, I hustled down to the Fill with a renewed feeling of gratitude for the beauty that exists all around us, but most particularly at my favorite place on Earth. Gray skies? Who cares when a tiny glob of sunlight glows in the heart of a green bush, and you realize you're looking straight at the orange head-feathers of an Orange-crowned Warbler? Cold breeze? How can that matter when you hear the sweet song of a Western Meadowlark floating on that very wind, drawing you to the fruit tree in the middle of Hunn Meadow West, where—wonder of wonders—the sunniest of all the prairie birds has thrown back his head to let his song peal forth? Gloom and doom simply cannot stand against the sweet symphony of browns in counterpoint with yellow bill and legs that is a Sora at his finest. Or the comic sight of three Solitary Sandpipers clustered together at the south end of Shoveler's Pond, glaring and nipping at each other because hello! Solitary Sandpipers are supposed to be solitary.

It is a great mystery why some people with severe physical disabilities or trauma come up smiling time after time, while others, with much smaller burdens to bear, feel hopelessly weighted down. My 97-year-old Aunt Marie used to say it was a matter of temperament. "Some people are just born sunny, and others are cloudy," she told me, on a day when I was feeling particularly stormy.

Marie was one of the sunny ones. Nothing seemed to get her down. Perhaps her optimism came from the fact that she never worried about anything. I remember one example, a time when she swooped down upon my dorm room to spirit me away. "We're going on a cruise down the Nile," she announced. She would treat me to such trips about once every seven years or so. On this occasion, she figured an Egyptologist would make a good guide, so she offered to take me along.

We flew into London on the night before we were supposed to catch our flight to Cairo, where we were to board the cruise ship that was sailing the next day. At the hotel, we set two alarm clocks, on my insistence, so we would be sure to wake up in time to catch the bus to Heathrow Airport.

Next morning, the clocks duly blared us awake. Methodically, we followed our list of things to do and arrived at the bus station in plenty of time. We boarded the bus that said "Heathrow" on its overhead sign, and waited. No one else was on the bus. We waited some more. No one came. Finally, I said to Marie, "Something is wrong. The bus should be leaving soon. Where is everyone?"

Marie told me to get a grip, but by now, my worry centers were cranking out adrenaline like a fire hose. I jumped out and snagged a man in uniform. "Do you know when the bus leaves for the airport?" I asked him.

"Blimey," he said, "not for another two hours yet. The first bus left an hour ago."

What?! I looked at the clock in the station. It was an hour later than we thought. Unbeknownst to us, the Brits had celebrated day-

Orange-crowned Warbler © Doug Parrott

light savings time in the dead of the previous night. Grabbing our bags, we ran out to the street, flagged a taxi, and told the driver we would give him £50 if he could get us to the airport in 30 minutes. Turning off his "taxi for hire" sign, he pulled his cap down, gripped the steering wheel with hands of iron, and put pedal to the metal. I will never forget that ride. I think there were at least two times when we hit bumps and became airborne.

At the airport, we ran up to the ticket booth, muttering apologies to the people waiting patiently in line. The airlines people recognized we were the latecomers to the party of 50 who were already on the plane. Shoving our boarding passes at us they said, "Run."

We did, bags flapping. People parted before us like the Red Sea, urging us onward with cheers and whistles. We arrived at the gate just as the steward was closing the door. "You're here at last," he said in as disgusted a tone as an Englishman could ever mutter and let us through. We fled down the tunnel and panted our apologies to the airline personnel and all the passengers as we sat down in the last two empty seats. The plane was already taxiing away from the gate by the time we had fastened our seat belts and got our breath back. I put my head down, hoping the black spots that floated all around my eyes would go away soon.

"Well," grinned my aunt, "that wasn't so bad, was it?"

Our little adventure happened 40 years ago, and I can still feel my mouth curl up into a smile whenever I think about it. Time, filled with events both good and bad, has since eroded my youth and taken my aunt away. And yet here I am. Still standing. Still laughing. A product of everything that has brought me to this moment and given me the insight to know at last how to answer my aunt's question: No, Marie, that wasn't so bad. In fact, it was funny. Charming. Great. Like life when you live it on the sunny side.

Despite the gray skies this spring, the wildflowers are blooming in Yesler Swamp, the Wood Ducks are outrageous, Great Blue Herons are everywhere, and sunlight fills my soul. May it fill yours as well.

13. Nuance

In my seventh decade, I have come to love the plain birds, the ones whose quiet feathers only whisper their beauty. It has taken me years to reach this point. When I was younger, I was captivated by color. I would stand stock-still at Main Pond, transfixed by the iridescent kaleidoscope of a male Wood Duck, the sunburst of a Yellow Warbler, the glowing orange and black embers of a Bullock's Oriole.

None of these birds have lost a particle of their beauty, but now they seem too obvious to me, too easy to appreciate. I prefer the challenge of finding the charm in dull birds such as the Say's Phoebe who has been enchanting me this past week at the Youth Farm.

Say's Phoebes are about as drab as drab can get. They are dirt brown on top, with slightly blacker caps and tails, dark gray on the breast, rusty brown farther below. They are adapted to blend in with the muted colors of the dry lands of the desert, where they make their living by catching flies. They perch on low structures and dash out to snag a bug on the wing. Then they return to their perch, wag their tails a while, and look for the next bite.

Say's Phoebes are among the first migrants to come back to our state, arriving in late February when the weather is still cold enough to coat the flora with frost. Most of them go to eastern Washington, where they can find plenty of early-hatching insects to catch among the sagebrush. But every now and then, one pays us a visit here on the wet side. This year's phoebe has been hanging out around the uplands of the Fill for the past week.

I saw it first on account of the kindness of birders. I was walking back to my car after a long stroll around the Fill, when two birders

Say's Phoebe at the Youth Farm ©Gregg Thompson

stopped me just short of the parking lot to ask me about a bird they wanted me to identify. Usually when people describe "a bird they have seen," I'm pretty hopeless at identifying what species it was. The observers' field marks are often sketchy and sometimes so far out of date I wonder whether the bird has become extinct by now—hence my inability to recognize it—or whether the observers' faulty memory has added a new, imaginary species to the list of North American birds. I nod as they give field marks that could apply to many different species, all of which I name, and none of which are ever correct.

This pair of birders, though, was highly precise. "From its behavior, it was a flycatcher for sure," one said. "It would fly out, catch an insect, fly back, and wag its tail. But we weren't sure exactly what kind of flycatcher. They're all pretty drab, you know. This one had a dark cap, dark tail, and russet belly."

Russet belly? I woke up. "When did you see it?" I asked despairingly. A Say's Phoebe—he of the belly so beautiful—had been spotted earlier in the week near the greenhouses southeast of the Center for Urban Horticulture, but I had missed it. I expected these two birders to name a date many days ago, adding to my misery and chagrin. I haven't seen a Say's Phoebe at the Fill in four years, and I was still chapped about missing the one at the greenhouses.

"When was it?" echoed the woman. "I don't know. Maybe five minutes ago?" Her husband nodded at me, but I was no longer there. My legs had begun to rotate like a jet turbine as I roared off down the trail. I think I might have left a small sonic boom behind.

Of course, by the time I got to the field—only 20 paces away!—the phoebe was no longer there. "Oh no, not again," I groaned. Gritting my teeth in a rictus of determination, I unfolded my camp stool. "I'm just going to sit here until that bird comes back," I said aloud grimly to the bird gods, "even if it takes a year. Or two. John can bring me food and a tarp."

Luckily, the phoebe came winging over my head in only ten minutes. It perched on a farm structure, cocked its head at me, and went about its business of catching flies. I did too—my mouth opened in a big oh of delight and stayed that way, inviting all and sundry insects to come on in.

The Sun appeared from behind the clouds and shone on this little bird like a benediction. I could see every feather of its nutmeg back, its cinnamon belly and peppery tail, a spice bird of the south come to season our spring. Queen Isabella paid out a fortune for Columbus to discover a quick route to the spices she craved; I got mine for free.

Since then, I have seen this Say's Phoebe several more times. Whenever I do, I am stopped in my tracks. The subtle play of its brown and charcoal feathers glows in the sunshine, and I am enthralled. One day, the Say's Phoebe flew out from the Youth Farm and hovered over a remnant stem of Queen Anne's Lace that was hosting a hatch of insects. As the phoebe picked off its prey one by one, it quivered in the air, wings outspread like a dark angel, heavenly beauty come to Earth for a brief stay.

Recently, I have been helping my daughter study for the GREs, a standardized test given to students before they apply to graduate school. My daughter is working to improve her vocabulary by studying lists of synonyms. English is not her native language, and she needs to expand her working knowledge of words. It hasn't been easy. "Why does English have so many words that mean the same thing?" she asked one day, exasperated by the similarity of "gullible" and "credulous," not to mention "loquacious" and "garrulous."

I struggled to explain the differences in nuance, but since I didn't understand them myself, I didn't get very far. "Let's think about the roots," I suggested. "'Credulous' comes from the Latin for 'to believe.' A credulous person believes whatever he or she hears. 'Gullible' comes from the Old English word 'gull,' meaning to trick. A gullible person is easily tricked. You can see that both words describe a person who is vulnerable to scams and deceit, but not quite in the same way."

Explaining the roots to my daughter, I explained them to myself. For the first time in my life, I saw the real but slight difference between these words. I realized how rich the English language is, a language that springs from three mighty rivers of human thought:

Greek, Latin, and German. It is a language that continues to accept new words—and new concepts—from around the world.

What a gift for a writer! But it is a gift with strings attached, for it means we writers must pay close attention to precision. Words that seem interchangeable may not be identical. There can be subtle differences. What fun to pay attention to such slightness, to fall in love with fine distinctions.

I suppose that's why I also fell in love with the subtlety of a Say's Phoebe. I have come to appreciate nuance. Perhaps this is a gift of age. To understand nuance, we have to move away from the black-and-white starkness of adolescence. This takes time. Over the years, as we experience the many shades of gray that color real life, we painfully learn how the world really works, rather than how we think it should work.

This awakening to reality sometimes produces bitterness in the young—especially for those who are idealistic—because the world can work so unfairly, and misery is everywhere on display. People are not always who they claim to be, and the promises of adults—about the rewards of hard work and the triumph of goodness—are often broken.

When older people who remember their own transition into the real world see this newfound cynicism of the young, they try to offer comfort, but it is often comfort of the cold kind. "Whoever said the world was fair?" they ask. "Or kind?" Those who lost their illusions long ago and became bitter are glad to welcome new company into their misery.

But as truthful as the cynics are, they do not possess all the truth. They lack hope, and they have no faith in unconditional love. In the end, their understanding of the world is too shallow. Somehow, we must find a way to accept the world as it is and love it just the same.

For me, finding the nuanced beauty in a superficially drab Say's Phoebe is a way to deepen my understanding of the world. When my breath is taken away by this plain brown bird—who eats flies, for Pete's sake—I learn I must actively and with effort look past the conventional and beneath the surface to find the beauty within.

And as I venture more deeply into the complexities of beauty, as I embrace nuance, with all its ambiguity and richness, I see that almost nothing is altogether bad or good. There are shades of meaning wherever we look. Redemption is possible for deeds most foul; acceptance of imperfection tempers the most righteous.

The world is both beautiful and ugly, but even in its ugliness, beloved.

Cooper's Hawk with prey: a yellow-shafted Northern Flicker. The flicker managed to get away when the hawk lifted its foot. ©Tim Kuhn

14. That's Tough

The Brewer's Blackbirds are at it again this spring over at the helipad. Several years ago, a little breeding colony started up in the bushes covering the fence that surrounds the airstrip. Since then, the blackbirds have returned every April to make new blackbirds.

Brewer's Blackbirds are insouciant avians whose ability to tolerate disturbance is unparalleled, in my experience. Take their choice of nesting sites. Of all the places at the Fill where they could have chosen to build their nests, they picked the noisiest and most active. When a helicopter flies in with a sick or injured child bound for Seattle Children's Hospital, all the blackbirds do in response is jump to the ground, face into the wind, and kind of squint till the rotors stop kicking up dust. They don't flee. When crows show up in search of tasty eggs or hatchlings, the blackbirds come boiling out of their bunkers to attack. I've seen them flap up to a soaring Bald Eagle and peck its innocent back. The eagle, while big, seems harmless to Brewer's Blackbirds, but that doesn't deter the blackbirds. Nothing seems to faze them.

I did become concerned for them this past year. The UW has built a varsity track in the south half of the blackbirds' field. The track was installed here after it was displaced by the renovation of Husky Stadium. Football fans wanted to sit closer to the field so they could more nearly become part of the football action, but the old track blocked access. It had to go, but where? The Powers That Be decided the blackbirds' field made the best choice, despite the fact that the field rests on multiple layers of rotting garbage, and below that, the deepest peat in the state. To keep the track from undulating like a motocross raceway on this squishy land, construction workers drove dozens of 60-foot-long metal piles into the muck. Theoretically, the track "floats," suspended on these foundation piles.

It's a miracle of engineering, but I can't help but be reminded of King Sneferu of Egypt. Sneferu was the first king of the Fourth Dynasty (ca. 2600 B.C.E.) and undoubtedly wanted to be remembered as a great ruler. How, though, was he going to outdo his greatest predecessor, King Djoser, who built the world's first pyramid? Prior to King Djoser, all the kings of Egypt were buried in one-story stone mansions resembling ranch houses, only with no windows. Djoser's architect got the idea of stacking one mansion on top of another, each layer a bit smaller than the one below, like a giant, tiered wedding cake. The result was the Step Pyramid.

Although the records don't tell us, I suspect King Sneferu suffered from pyramid envy. Imagine, every time he visited the state cemetery at Saqqara, he had to look at the monstrous symbol of a previous king, looming over the capital like a giant billboard proclaiming Djoser's superiority. That's got to gripe a guy. So Sneferu ordered an even larger pyramid for himself.

Sneferu's pyramid started out as a step pyramid, too. But Sneferu wasn't satisfied with just showing off his greater size. He must have worried that he might still be out-tombed by his predecessor, who after all, had been first with the step idea. So Sneferu ordered his minions to come up with a totally new idea.

Some unnamed genius suggested filling in the steps with rubble and sticking on an outer casing of smooth limestone to create the world's first true pyramid. Sneferu loved the idea and ordered the work to begin immediately. Unfortunately, the architect in charge didn't know how to build such a newfangled structure and made the angle of the limestone casing too steep. The façade began to slide off, creating a mountain of rubble that still encircles the shapeless core to this day. Not the memorial Sneferu had in mind.

Ordinarily, a goof the size of this one would have meant the end of the project and possibly the end of the architect. However, Sneferu was not a quitter. Instead, he ordered another pyramid to be built. This time, he was determined to build a smooth-sided pyramid from the get-go. No steps. Unfortunately, the same lack of knowledge about gravity that had done in the first design was still lacking on the second, and the angles were once again too steep. When it became clear that the limestone casing would go the way of Sneferu's first pyramid, the architect altered the last third of the structure to slope more gently, thus creating the Bent Pyramid.

An architect friend of mine once told my sixth-grade writing students about the difference between architecture and art. "If an artist makes a mistake," he said, "he or she can erase it, or paint over it, or maybe even throw the work away. If an architect makes a mistake, it's there for all the world to see."

Sneferu would no doubt have agreed. Rather than a testimonial to his greatness, the Bent Pyramid's message was one giant "Oops."

Back to the drawing board, with the result that Sneferu commissioned a third pyramid. This time, everyone got it right. Today the Red Pyramid still stands, an enormous human-made mountain of carved sandstone blocks rising from the desert at Dahshur. Upon completion, it was the tallest structure ever constructed. I can imagine the pleased pharaoh standing proudly in front of his monument, arms akimbo, eyes shining. "Now that's what I call a pyramid."

A huge structure of similar cutting-edge architecture has risen in the blackbirds' field. It doesn't have the grandeur of a pyramid, but its engineering principles are as cutting-edge today as the Red Pyramid was 4,600 years ago. I hope for the sake of the architects it is not a big oops that will eventually sag as droopily as Sneferu's first effort.

"How can you say that?" a birder friend asked me the other day after I had bloviated about the new track and its similarities to old Egyptians. "The architects have destroyed more than half of the blackbirds' field. Why would you want it to succeed? Wouldn't it make more sense to hope the track subsides until it becomes useless as a varsity facility? Wouldn't that teach everyone not to build on this unstable land? Wouldn't that do more to preserve the rest of the

Fill forever?" I could see my friend's blood pressure rising. "What's wrong with you, anyway?"

His voice rang with conviction. I could feel my inner Che Guevara rising in response, Yeah, that's what we want. Failure on a colossal scale. That'll teach 'em. Why, I ought to hold a student rally, march over to the track, protest signs a-waving, lie down on the site and lock arms, threatening to stay until the university agrees to remove this monstrous blot on nature.

Then my revolutionary fervor fades. Not from age, I hope, but more because I know the blackbirds will survive. We nibbled away at the edges of their habitat, but the core survives. For now.

I also know something else. Preserving nature will take more than a few student rallies and a little American-style tea party. We cannot keep fighting the same battle—evil developer vs. shining

Brewer's Blackbird © Tim Kuhn

knight enviro—over and over. It's too hard to sound the battle cry time and again, too patchy to win a little skirmish here and there, too impermanent. To really make a difference, we must change the very way we relate to nature itself. We must change ourselves, both from within and from without.

Change from within means we must change the way we define the good life for ourselves. Our values drive our decisions, and that is why we must each think very carefully about how we want to live and how much it will cost us in terms of resources. Will the good life for us continue to mean untrammeled consumption, or can we redefine happiness and success in other terms? When we make choices about how to be stewards of the land, will we continue to put our own needs and pleasures first, or will we sublimate our needs to those of nature? How much will we value the wild—enough to leave it alone when it harbors something we want or need?

Unless we place a higher value on the nature we have right now, we will continue to alter the ecological balance that has taken eons to establish. Nature will survive, but it won't be same nature. Will we like the new balance as much as the old? Probably not, because environmental effects caused by humans happen fast, and evolution works slowly. Niches left empty by an extinct species will not be filled quickly. Exotic species introduced by climate change and human activity will eventually harmonize with the native species, but not before wreaking havoc for generations. Most of the changes occurring now will therefore be recorded on the loss side of the ledger, not the gain side.

We must also recognize that changing our values will not be enough to preserve our planet in its present natural state. We must also change from without, meaning we must change our policies. The world is becoming ever more interconnected, with globalized systems of production and consumption. Such planet-scale integration requires a similar scale of cooperation on issues that face us all: overpopulation, global climate change, unsustainable growth in consumption, weapons of mass destruction, water shortages, energy shortages, food shortages, uneven distribution of resources.

These planet-wide problems will not be solved just by me walking my little way to work every day instead of driving, or growing my own tomatoes instead of buying the ones grown in Mexico. While individual efforts can have widespread effects, even if you multiply "me" by several million, the scale is too small, the systems too complex. Instead, we must be willing to regulate ourselves globally, on an even larger scale than individual nations.

Can we do it? Surely the answer is yes. We have the tools we need right now to tackle these problems head-on and solve them. Tools, however, are not enough. We need commitment. Attitude. The sheer bloody-mindedness of the blackbird.

Many years ago, when my husband was a young man, he went to work for his father in a farm supply business. It was a shoestring operation. John's dad did not have the money to buy good equipment or reliable delivery vehicles. He often sent John out in a truck without brakes to deliver dangerous chemicals to waiting farmers who had little patience for excuses.

One day, John was driving a particularly rickety old truck when one of the near-bald tires hit a rock in the road and exploded. John pulled over to change the tire, but the nuts were so old they seemed welded to their threads. He tried to twist them off, leaning his whole weight onto the tire iron, to no effect. He struggled for more than an hour, but the nuts wouldn't budge. Finally, he heard another truck chugging down the road. It was his younger brother, come to see what was causing the delay.

Bob got out to watch his brother give another twist to the tire iron. "Did you know those nuts go on backwards?" he asked.

John stopped working. "You mean I've spent the last hour tightening them?" he asked incredulously.

Bob started to laugh. Then John started to laugh. They were laughing so hard they had to lean against each other to keep from falling over. Finally, wiping the tears streaming down his face, John grabbed the tire iron and turned it the correct way. Nothing moved. John is a strong man, and he had spent an hour tightening those nuts to superhuman levels of tightness. Bob took a turn but did no better.

The two young men stood there in the hot sun, wondering what to do. Then Bob grabbed the tire iron and heaved a mighty heave. Sweat poured off his brow. Grunts came from the depths of his belly as he put all he had into the effort, as he put more than he had, as he strained against the immovable. "You won't do it," said John. "You can't get that nut off."

But Bob wouldn't give up. "This nut is going to come off because it *has* to come off," he panted. It did.

We require a healthy ecosystem to survive. Therefore, at some point, we are going to preserve nature because we *have* to preserve nature. But in finally doing what is necessary to preserve enough nature to keep the air pure, the water fresh, the food available, will we wait until we have lost so much we can no longer recognize the planet we have? Environmentalists the world over answer this question with a resounding "No." None of us have waited for anything. On the contrary, we have pushed ahead in the face of inertia and opposition. But we are not enough. We must be joined by a majority of the planet's people, and most especially, by those who define what it means to live the good life.

The blackbirds do everything they can to hang onto their nest site at the helipad. They do so because they are tough survivors who have the flexibility to tolerate human activity to a high degree. Not every species is as tough. Nor are the blackbirds infinitely flexible. After a few weeks of putting up with the construction noise, the dust, and the near-constant human activity last year, the blackbirds finally threw in the towel and left. This March, six came back to check out their old nesting site. I saw them perched on the helipad fence, their eyes squinting into the stiff breeze. I think they will stick around and try to nest again, but there are limits to the strain we put on them and on the environment.

Let us be honest with ourselves and admit those limits exist. Then let us be tough-minded enough to do what it takes in both our private lives and our planetary policies to live within them. Happiness, after all, is not measured—or granted—by our outer limits but by our inner spirit.

15. Two Elusive Dreams

I was pussyfooting on the trail near the east side of Southeast Pond the other day, in an attempt to spot the Virginia Rail who has been calling to her chicks recently. Virginia Rails are shy marsh birds who breed in the Fill wherever a dense patch of cattails offers them sufficient cover. I've heard them calling from nine different locations this year, but I have yet to see one.

Part of the problem is that Virginia Rails abhor being looked at, so they almost never come out from behind the cattails of their marsh. I used to be able to peer into the marsh around the pond over the tops of the reeds and spot the occasional rail, but the cattails here have grown higher than my head this year, and I can no longer see the water at all, much less any rails.

Luckily for me, this morning the Virginia Rail who claims the pond as her territory had left her sanctuary and was calling plaintively from amongst the grass stems of the upland prairie to the north. She was way out of her comfort zone, and I knew it wouldn't be long before this Marco Polo of the rail clan would realize it and come back to her proper milieu. All I had to do was wait, and eventually I would see her little body scuttle across the trail.

Cautiously, I unslung my camp stool and bent over to set it down on the verge. Without warning, there was an explosive whir at my feet, and a brown body with a preposterously long bill rocketed out of the verdure.

"Aaahhh!" I screamed, as my heart attempted to displace the larynx in my throat. Adrenalin poured through my arteries, raising their vascular pressure to a level previously thought to be impossible. My camp stool shot out of my hands and arched into the next field, like a caber tossed by an overachieving Scot.

Every bird in the immediate vicinity dove into hiding, leaving the Fill empty of all visible animal life, except for one reeling birder clutching her chest. Eventually, after replacing my heart and retrieving my errant stool, I wended my way down the trail, all possibility of finding a rail as vanished as the rail itself. I had just seen my first-of-the-year Wilson's Snipe.

Wilson's Snipes are every bit as elusive as rails. Snipes are freshwater shorebirds with short legs and Jimmy Durante beaks. They use their long schnozzolas to probe soft mud for worms and burrowing insects. The bills are loaded with sensitive nerves at the tips to feel for a likely morsel.

Wilson's Snipes are themselves a favorite food item on the menu of many raptors who frequent the Fill, including Peregrine Falcons, Merlins, Cooper's Hawks, Sharp-shinned Hawks, and even Red-tails. No wonder snipes are wary.

They are not without defenses, however. Nature has equipped Wilson's Snipes with eyes near the tops of their heads, so they can spot danger from above. They also have cryptically colored feathers. A snipe can blend in with its marsh and grassland habitat so perfectly you can look right at one and not see it, at least, not until you scare it enough so it flies away. That's why most birders are more familiar with the back ends of Wilson's Snipes than with the whole bird.

I'd been looking for both Virginia Rails and Wilson's Snipes for weeks. I knew they were here, if only they would show themselves. Sometimes, as I searched diligently in all the likely spots, glassing each cattail clump with my binoculars until my arms ached, I could feel them watching me. Teasing me with their calls. Mocking me by wiggling an occasional reed. Laughing at me.

"Richard Nixon used to talk about folks laughing at him, too," said my husband when I told him this theory. "He put them on his enemies list."

"It's not paranoia I'm talking about," I answered, eyeing my husband suspiciously. Was he *laughing* at me? "It's Borges."

In 1947, Jorge Luis Borges wrote a short story about the famous Arab philosopher Averroes, who, Borges imagined, tried to translate Aristotle's *Poetics.* Averroes failed because he couldn't understand the meaning of the words "tragedy" or "comedy." There was no such thing as a play in Averroes's Islamic culture, which forbade the depiction of human beings.

In the course of his long search, says Borges, Averroes told himself he shouldn't give up. On the contrary, he should keep looking

Wilson's Snipe © Doug Parrott

because the answer was near. "Whatever you seek, it is never far away," he quotes.

That's just what I have been telling myself for weeks now. I seek the rail and the snipe, and I know they are not far away. I know if I am patient, if I show up every day, rain or shine, and keep looking, I will find what I seek. I have faith.

Most people who quote Borges's saying, though, are talking about a different kind of faith—faith in the divine grace of God. It has been a great comfort to people down through the ages to know that such grace is near, to know if you seek it, you will find it.

Many other things in life are similarly accessible, as I explained to my husband, if only we open our hearts to them. Love, friendship, kindness, wisdom, happiness—all are nearby, within reach, available to everyone. They may seem impossible to find at times, but they all exist within the human heart, and so they are always near to us. As near as those darned snipes and rails.

"That's not what Borges meant at all," my husband said, interrupting the flow of my bloviation river. I had been in full spate, but John's objection stopped me like a lockmaster slamming shut the floodgates. "Borges was actually being quite cynical," John explained. "'Whatever you seek is never very far away' means that human beings are completely incapable of imagining anything dramatically creative. Borges was saying that we can think only of little improvements, little dreams, the things that are close to what we already know."

Then John looked at me with narrowed eyes. "Borges wasn't being hopeful at all. You didn't really read his story, did you?"

"All right, so I couldn't get through it," I admitted. "You know as well as I do Borges is too abstract for me. Give me a good murder mystery where the butler really did it. So what?"

John explained that Borges's story ends with an image of Averroes staring into a mirror and then suddenly and mysteriously disappearing. Borges confesses his whole story was a dream he created to illustrate failure: Borges's own failure to imagine the real Islamic philosopher Averroes out of the small fragments of history that are all we have left of him.

"Borges wanted to acknowledge the limits of human imagination, and thus the limits of human achievement," said John. "But I reject that utterly."

John went on to talk about the leaps of discovery he admires most: the thinkers who conceived of the Enlightenment; the people who invented the scientific method, which has done so much to unlock the secrets of the universe; the artists who have envisioned worlds as yet unseen; the composers who heard celestial music in their minds and wrote it down for the rest of us. John has studied the lives of these people because he seeks to understand how they did it. He wants to learn from their examples so he can achieve at that level himself.

John's contribution to creative science is a molecular imager. Years ago, he began theorizing a technology that would image atoms by detecting the direction of their minute magnetic spins. He wanted to create a device that would enable us to see molecules in situ so we can understand the ecology of a cell, an ecology that exists like a tiny world within a world. By doing so, John hopes he and his fellow scientists can persuade cells to regenerate damaged or lost tissue: to restore health to injured nerves, help paralyzed people walk, heal diseases that are untreatable now.

To make such a big dream come true, John needs all his hope. That's why he rejects Borges. He can't afford to listen to naysayers, no matter how literary they are. John believes the only thing that can truly stop us from turning our dreams into reality is if we stare into the mirror of ourselves and see only the limitations. Because then the possibilities of who we can become disappear, and nothing is left but the person we are today. How boring is that?

Every day I go to the Fill, I begin my walk with unbounded anticipation. Who knows what the wind blew in the night before? Birds do fly. There could be a rare surprise waiting just around the corner, a new species appearing at the Fill for the very first time, or a common bird showing some new behavior. I want to see it all, everything, both the new birds I've never seen before and the old ones I've seen a hundred times before. I want to feel it all: the supreme, unbreakable connection I make to nature, and through nature, to something larger and more eternal than I am. When I make that connection, I am changed.

I have no wish to stay the same. I hope I never stop becoming. I hope I never stop dreaming about new possibilities. For it is with such dreams that we create the true reality of our lives—not the mundane facts of everyday existence we all endure, but the soaring possibility of what we alone can give to the world: ourselves. With our dreams, we shape our future.

Killdeer nest with chicks and an egg © Evan Houston

16. Winners

Hidden away between the back entrance of the baseball diamond and Canal Road is a tiny pool of water that stands deserted all week long. Few people know of it, certainly not the construction workers and athletic department vehicle-drivers who make the road a noisy thoroughfare from Monday through Saturday. On Sundays, though, when the workers stay home, the American Goldfinches come to this pool to take a bath.

Not that goldfinches are shy bathers, mind you. On the contrary, they are quite willing to bathe in public, plashing their wings in any convenient puddle as they scatter glistening droplets of water far and wide. But they are also aware that bathing can be a dangerous activity. In the exuberance of the bath, they can forget to look out for predators. That's why they like the seclusion of the hidden pool.

They are wise to be wary.

I was sitting on my camp stool one recent spring morning, enjoying the flash of gold birds and silvery water as seven finches bathed, when out of nowhere rocketed an American Kestrel on the hunt. Squealing in terror, the goldfinches sprang into the air, desperate to get away. For a nanosecond, the scene was filled with churning birds, a bewildering kaleidoscope of yellow finches and chestnut kestrel. Then the circle of birds rolled apart, with finches scattering in all directions as the kestrel powered down the road.

I tried to catch my breath. Everything had happened so fast. As I looked around at the now-deserted road, I felt confused, partly by the speed of the attack, and partly by the uncertainty and ambiguity of the outcome. Did the kestrel capture its prey, or did the prey escape? Whenever I witness such attacks by raptors, I am glad when the prey is safe, but sad when the raptor misses a meal.

Kestrels are our smallest falcon. They need to catch something to eat every day to survive. Back when farm fields and open spaces dominated the landscape of King County, catching prey used to be easy for the kestrels. There was plenty of habitat for their favorite food: crickets, grasshoppers, voles, mice, and small birds. The falcons would perch on top of telephone poles or wires—conveniently located along nearly every road bordering the farms—and wait for something interesting to come out into the open. Sometimes they would hover over a field as they searched, their wings flapping furiously, their heads absolutely still.

When I began birding the Fill in the 1980s, American Kestrels dependably showed up every fall and winter. Usually they favored a wooden pole standing on the northwest corner of Main Pond. There, they would survey the prairie below and pick out likely prey to pounce upon. But sometime during the 1990s, the pole fell down, and our prairie was gradually replaced by invasive blackberry. Meanwhile, in the rural valleys of King County more than 70 percent of the farmland became asphalt. Kestrels grew scarce.

American Goldfinches, on the other hand, became common. Hardly a day goes by when I do not see them somewhere at the Fill. In summer, they come in large flocks to dine on thistle. In winter, the alder cones draw them here in even bigger numbers.

You might conclude from this data that in the Darwinian contest of "survival of the fittest," goldfinches are winning and kestrels are losing. And you would be right, at least in King County, at least in this newly hatched century. On the other hand, you could also point to the fact that both goldfinches and kestrels have declined compared to their populations 50 years ago, and therefore, both species are losing. Ruh-roh. On still another hand, 200 years ago most of King County was heavily forested, and there were almost no kestrels or goldfinches; both species have increased astronomically since then, so they're winning. Of course, 15,000 years ago, the land hereabouts lay under a half-mile-thick sheet of ice and there were no birds of any sort, so holy smokes, look at the trend lines since then!

As I pondered these complexities, the goldfinches returned and gradually resumed their interrupted bath, as though nothing had happened. One of them even closed her eyes as she splashed, apparently unworried that Nemesis might return. Such insouciance was way beyond my powers. Heck, I'm still wary about taking showers when I'm alone in the house, on account of seeing Alfred Hitchcock's movie *Psycho,* and that was more than 50 years ago.

Idly, I counted the finches in the puddle. Seven, just as before. All the finches had eluded the kestrel, despite the fact that some had leaped into the air more belatedly than others and had lagged behind in the race to get away.

I realized that the notion of "survival of the fittest" is probably too strict a measuring rod to determine the winners and losers in the Darwinian evolution game. "Survival of the fit enough" works just as well, especially if you're accounting only for individuals and their brief life spans.

That is good news for a philosopher like me who looks to nature for lessons on how to lead the good life. For a long time now, I have wanted to turn away from the notion that relentless competition is what characterizes all interactions in nature, and by inference, all human interactions, too. I have been searching instead for a natural law that is kinder and more inclusive than "winner take all."

Not that I hate competition. On the contrary, when I was younger, I lived for competitive sports. I lettered in volleyball, softball, and badminton in each of my four years in college. In fact, my husband and I solidified our relationship on the badminton courts, where I never let him win more than three points against me, even though my mother counseled me, "Let him win a few. Guys don't like it when girls beat them." As if.

When my kids were old enough to start playing games with me, however, I discovered winning was not the be-all of my existence, as I had thought. I learned this on the day my two sons, ages five and three, burst into tears when I crushed them playing "Candy Land."

"What's the matter with you?" my husband demanded. "They're toddlers! Can't you let them win at least once?"

This baffled me. Why play a game and not try your hardest to win? If I *let* my kids win, wouldn't that teach them wrong lessons about how the world works? I couldn't imagine Darwin ever throwing a game for his kids.

But as I grew older, I found myself becoming less interested in beating the competition. Maybe that's because now that my kids are grown, they can beat me in any sport! I hope, though, that it's really because I have grown in wisdom and no longer value the simple-mindedness of the traditional definition of winning. For in our vocabulary, winning usually means coming out on top, being the first to cross the finish line, the one to jump the highest, throw the farthest, gain the most points.

I used to care so much about all that. Maybe I still would, if I had competed at the Olympics level. Maybe if I had had to train as hard as Olympians do and sacrifice as much, I would think it sublime

American Goldfinches taking a bath ©Doug Parrott

American Kestrel © Thomas Sanders

to compete with—and beat—the best in all the world. Perhaps on that day, as I raised my hands in victory, the triumph would all be worth it. Later, as the years went by, I'd keep my medal polished and pristine behind a glass case, to be hauled out on rare occasions to show the kids and grandkids. "Wow, Grandma," they'd say, "were you really that good?" They'd look at my decrepit body and think, "If she could do it, maybe we can, too," and another generation of competitors would be born. Maybe in that alternate universe, I'd ask that my medal be hung around my neck as I lay in my casket, so eons from now, when future archaeologists dig up the necropolis of Evergreen Washelli, they'd find me with my medal and think I was some kind of queen. The Queen of Badminton. Scientists would be intrigued. Was Badminton a realm? A title? An entire people? Papers would be written debating the likelihood of each treasured thesis. I and my golden hoard would be famous down through the ages, though my name would be lost in the mists of time.

In reality, though, I never achieved an Olympian level of proficiency in any of my sports. I was never willing to work that hard or sacrifice that much. I was never that good, to be honest. Few people are. Most of us, when you come right down to it, compete in sports for fun. We learn it is more fun to win than to lose, more fun to bring home a trophy than to come home empty-handed, although I must say that in the days when I competed, women didn't get too many shiny trophies. The trophy I won for my biggest badminton tournament, a state-wide competition in Illinois, was a feathered shuttlecock pasted upside-down on a round piece of cardboard. The business end of the shuttlecock was decorated with fake hair and had a little face painted on it. It was supposed to be a Southern belle dressed in a full-length ball gown made of feathers. To this day, I have no idea what the tournament sponsors were thinking of.

My husband John was a little more fortunate. He had never competed in sports as a youth because his father needed him to work in the family business. But after grad school, John took up surfing. In 1982, he entered the Del Rey Surf Club competition for men aged 25 and over. Only two other guys entered that category, and one fell out of the competition when a wave made him lose his board. So John won second place. He was so proud when he received his trophy, a shiny red and gold plastic paean to sport. It has a little man on a pedestal with arms upraised. In one hand, the little man holds a laurel wreath. I presume he represents the ancient Greek ideal of the athlete. Above him is another man, a surfer on a surfboard, propelled by a static wave of golden plastic. The trophy is engraved with John's name: John Sidels. Sidels? The engraver had switched the "e" and the "l" in John's last name. A trophy with a typo.

I've often thought I should get a new engraving with John's name spelled correctly, but somehow, the original plaque seems to suit us a lot better. We're a family who don't take ourselves too seriously because we know fate is full of jokes, often at our expense. When fate lays a big one on us, we just have to laugh.

John and I have lived a life full of victories and defeats, as everyone has who has reached our age. We know what it feels like to win, and how often a win is not as thrilling as we thought it should be. We also know what it means to lose, and what it takes to pick ourselves back up and try again. Neither winning nor losing defines us anymore. Those ephemera have been replaced by something a lot more meaningful: Achievement of goals we set for ourselves, not those set by others. Fulfillment as we choose to shape it. Laughter every day. Love of family and friends.

It's a different world than the hypercompetitive one that popular culture tells us we all live in. That world demands losers as avidly as it rewards winners. It is one in which the desire to win infuses nearly everything people do, whether they're in business, politics, the classroom, entertainment, sports, even scientific research.

Furthermore, when we win, we're supposed to show everyone the proof that validates both our win and our selves. So we live in houses of such enormous size, they echo. We drive cars of such power, they roar. We wear spendy clothes, visit trendy resorts, eat fashion foods, appear in cool places, all to show the world what winners we are. The rest of the world watches and emulates, adding billions of competitors to the game. Now we have to beat people living halfway around the world, not just halfway down the block.

This view of globalization as one gigantic struggle to come out on top has taken over our minds partly because it seems so scientific. It's Darwinian nature. But human beings have great power to construct our own environment, especially when it comes to our culture and our relationships. Surely we have reached a point in our civilization where we no longer must live enslaved by the brutalities of raw nature. Surely we have the generosity and sense of community to redefine winning in such a way that allows more than just the fittest—and the few—to win, while the rest of us sink into oblivion.

Fred Rogers, of *Mr. Rogers' Neighborhood* fame, certainly thought so. He used to give commencement addresses to college seniors during which he would tell his favorite story. It was about a Special Olympics hundred-yard dash in which nine children competed.

"At the sound of the gun," said Rogers, "they all took off. But one little boy didn't get very far. He stumbled and fell and hurt his knee and began to cry. The other eight children heard the boy crying. They slowed down, turned around, and ran back to him—every one of them ran back to him. The little boy got up, and he and the rest of the runners linked their arms together and joyfully walked to the finish line.

"They all finished the race at the same time. And when they did, everyone in the stadium stood up and clapped and whistled and cheered for a long, long time. And you know why? Because deep down we know that what matters in this life is more than winning for ourselves. What really matters is helping others win, too, even if it means slowing down and changing our course now and then."

The denizens of nature are locked in an eternal contest to survive. To succeed, they must win out over their competitors as they seek food, water, mates, even a place to rest. They are engaged in an unforgiving struggle that rewards winners and crushes losers, a drama I witness every day at the Fill.

Birds such as the goldfinches and kestrel I watched this spring can't change the rules that govern their lives. But we can.

What a victory *that* would be.

Part III
Summer

17. Renaissance

Oh, to be a young robin, out in the world for the first time, finding your first worm, singing your first song!

It is early June, and the baby birds are beginning to leave their nests. Everywhere you look, there are youngsters flying around, some still attached to their parents like toddlers begging for a popsicle, others completely alone already.

You can tell the young birds apart from the adults because their field marks are different. Immature robins have black spots on their russet breasts. Their heads and faces are pale and tufty, making their pinkish bills stand out. The bills curve down slightly, like Charlie Brown making a face after his kite has been captured by the kite-eating tree for the bazillionth time.

But you don't really have to see a young robin's field marks to know it is young. Its utter cluelessness identifies it even from a distance. Young robins fly around in a doh-de-doh kind of world. They don't know when to hide or keep quiet. They aren't very good at spotting worms in the grass, or telling which fruit is ripe enough to eat. When they land on a perch, they often wobble, flapping their wings in a desperate attempt to regain their balance. No Wallenda would ever hire a young robin for the family's high wire act, despite the fact that juvenile birds can fly without a safety net.

And yet, young robins are the very essence of joy in nature. Their bright black eyes take in everything with a chirpy kind of interest that only the very young display. I was that young once—we all were—but it is hard to remember what it felt like to believe the whole world was one giant laboratory set up just for us to explore. Luckily, since all young children look at the world with wide-eyed wonder and are very willing to share their views with us, it's quite easy to recreate the sensation. All you have to do is snag a willing child and go out into nature together.

I do this regularly with preschoolers from a local daycare. The kids arrive in a van, accompanied by numerous adults. As soon as the van doors open and the kids are let out, they scatter in all directions, chased by us adults in a futile attempt to regain control. We flap our arms and cluck like chickens as we try to make our elderly legs move fast enough to catch up to the little tykes, but it's pretty hopeless.

Eventually, the kids get tired of running up and down the gravel trails. Their legs are short, you know, so they have to take at least three steps to our one. If we adults can just keep up the chase long enough without having to call 911, we can wear the little guys down and capture them.

I say "we adults," but really it's more accurate to say the teachers. I gave up participating in the chase after the first time, because I found that the resulting black spots floating in front of my eyes prevented me from identifying any birds. Now I let the teachers do the roundup. Some of the teachers are quite fleet, chasing down the kids and catching them on the run. Other teachers wait for the kids to get riveted by a bug crawling along on the ground; then the teachers calmly retrieve the preoccupied preschoolers. It's tempting to test the teachers in time trials to see which ones retrieve kids more quickly, but in the end, even the slowest teacher succeeds in rounding up her charges.

Once the class has reassembled, I tell the kids about the big bird who lives near the beaver tree down at East Point. This is a Great Blue Heron who has claimed the marsh here as her fishing hole. She comes every morning to hunt for frogs and fish, despite the fact that the heron must stand almost within touching distance of the people who pass by on the trail. I guess so many joggers and strollers stream by every day that the heron has ceased to be bothered by human

Juvenile American Robin © Tim Kuhn

activity. In fact, sometimes the heron strides out of the marsh and sashays down the trail like a svelte model until she reaches a break in the cattails, where she can re-enter the water. It's unnerving to come around the bend in the trail here and see this heron on the runway. But it's a great bird for kids to watch, so I always hope she's present.

"You have to be quiet when you get close to the marsh," I tell the kids, "and you have to move slowly. Otherwise, Big Bird will think you're about to frighten away the frogs and fish, and she'll leave."

One year, one of the little boys in the class was especially rambunctious. He was one of those kids who can't stay still for more than a nanosecond. He was a shouter, too. Even when the teachers told him to use his indoor voice, he produced enough volume to blow my hair back. The other kids all looked to him as a leader, not necessarily because he was loaded with charm or charisma, but mostly because he could be in six different places at once. I guess the kids figured anyone who could be that omnipresent might have high omnipotence potential as well, and omnipotent beings like to lead. Not that the kids would ever say so, of course.

When I made my speech about the need to be quiet, this little hurricane immediately told all the other kids to stop talking. Two girls ignored him because they were gossiping about something they thought was far more important, but when he speared them with a stern look, even they shut up. Then he got up on his toes and tiptoed all the way to the marsh, followed by all the other kids, also on tiptoe. I doubt the class had ever been so silent before.

The heron, unluckily, was not there. But a Bald Eagle had elected to perch on top of the wooden pole that juts up from the marsh only a few feet from the trail. When the kids rounded the bend and came face to face with the eagle, everyone froze, including the bird. After a few seconds, the eagle turned away regally to look out over the lake, allowing us to view its magnificence for long minutes. The children were awed.

So was I, but not by the eagle per se. I was struck instead by the connection the eagle made with the kids. It was almost as if the eagle was being deliberately tolerant of the young humans who so obviously admired it. This kind of encounter doesn't happen very often when I lead preschoolers. As a matter of fact, I've never seen an eagle on that post again. But every time I've led little kids to the Fill, some sort of connection happens. Often, it's a bug the kids connect with. Kids are a lot closer to the ground than I am, so it's no surprise they're more fascinated by insects.

When no bugs are present on the trail, no birds are in sight, and I'm fresh out of stories to tell, the kids turn to inanimate nature for inspiration. Puddles are a favorite, probably because a lot of the puddles at the Fill are iridescent, due to oily bubbles that come from the rotting garbage below ground. The kids don't understand the significance or irony of beauty created by pollution. They call them rainbow puddles. "Why do the puddles glow?" they ask me.

I don't know. It's something to do with diffraction or refraction, I imagine. Or maybe it's deflection. Reflection? I am completely clueless, so I shrug my shoulders.

Neither do I know the answer when a child asks me another typical toddler question: "Why do all the trees grow with their roots in the ground?"

I give the standard answer about how roots soak up water in the soil, allowing the tree to "drink," but then the kid says, "If trees use their roots to soak up water, wouldn't it be better for trees if their roots grew on top? That way, the trees could soak up more rain."

Again I shrug, feeling as ignorant—yet as wonderstruck—as any preschooler. The kids go back to exploring, and I wait for their next zinger. It is why I am here with them today. They are too young to know the restrictions the world will place on them, and so their view of the universe is like a giant cone of vision, expanding ever outward from their eyes into infinity, without limit. Seeing the universe through their eyes—seeing the infinite possibilities of life—my vision is expanded, too.

We adults place much value on knowledge. I suppose the more we know, the better we are able to predict the future. For creatures like us, who exist without natural defenses such as claws or sharp teeth, it's important to be able to make accurate predictions. We need to know whether to expect a leopard in the next tree, or a poisonous snake in the next grass tuft. We need to be able to identify patterns in the natural world that give us insight about what to expect in different situations so we can guard against disaster. The more exact our expectations, the safer we are.

But as helpful as expectations can be in guiding us to make good decisions for the future, they are a kind of oppression, too. When we have expectations for other people, we are really coercing them to do what we want them to do, or what we think is best for them—or maybe, what's best for us.

This can be a kindness at times—or even a necessity—for example, when I invite people over for dinner and say, "I'll expect you at 7." People like to know when they're supposed to arrive for a time-urgent event like a hot dinner. It is also a kindness in the long run for parents and teachers to set high expectations for youngsters. This is a way to encourage children to achieve more than they might think they can.

However, expecting others to do what we say requires that we can control what they do. We may indeed have some small measure of control over others, especially when it comes to bossing children around, but realistically, we're lucky if we can exert control over ourselves, much less anyone else.

Expectations for the world at large are just as problematic. They work when we have control over circumstances. They often let us down when we don't. For example, I can confidently expect my car to take me wherever I want to go, as long as the gas light hasn't been on for more than a few miles, and the engine doesn't make that funny smell. I may not control every working part of my car, but I can control the amount of gas I have in the tank and the frequency with which I get the oil changed. Thus, having car expectations is sensible. Having an AAA card is even more sensible for those times when the car gets the bit between its teeth and decides to act up without warning. Cars can sense when you're most vulnerable, you know, so I always keep my AAA dues paid. It's my way of controlling the beast.

Having expectations about world events that I cannot control, however, makes no sense at all. That's why it always drives me a little bit crazy when someone else spots a rare bird at the Fill and then hours later, posts it on Tweeters, the birders' online forum. Since I want to see every bird that visits the Fill, I run down there right away with the expectation that the bird will still be somewhere and I will be able to find it. Sometimes I do; often I don't. Either way, though, I have let myself be coerced by circumstance. Instead of feeling joy at the beauty of my surroundings, I feel anxiety about finding one tiny bird in 75 acres of foliage. I rush here, I rush there, searching for something that may or may not be present anymore. If I find the bird, I feel relief instead of joy. If I fail to find the bird, I feel deprived and disappointed.

It's much better to go the Fill without such expectations. Then, whatever I find is a thrill, whether it's a new bird, a new behavior, a new insight, an old friend, or a reminder of fond memory.

"Well, talk about setting the bar low for yourself," a friend said when I told him this. "Where's the ambition in life if you don't set expectations for yourself? Besides, you *do* have expectations. You've birded here long enough to know when to expect certain birds to show up in migration, and you know where to expect to see the ones that nest. You've kept records about that stuff for years. You have expectations up the wazoo—you just don't want to admit it."

Not being one who thinks fast on her feet, I kept silent. At the time, all I could think of to reply was, "Huh-uh," and that sounded juvenile. Now that I've had time to consider, I should have said that what I take to the Fill is anticipation, not expectation. Anticipation means I look forward to whatever I encounter. During spring migration, every new arrival validates for me the fact that the Earth is still more or less okay. Fall migration brings the year's newest birds my way, so I can celebrate the success of the breeding season. I am eager to see the old regulars in their usual places, if they choose to appear, because I like getting to know them as individuals. Every year when the winter residents leave, I feel a little sad at their departure but very glad to welcome the summer residents who take their place.

The difference between expectation and anticipation is the acceptance of my lack of power to control events. Letting go of the need to control everything allows me to be open to whatever nature does present. I am never disappointed, not because I set the bar of my expectations low but because nature always presents me with something surprising. Like the toddlers I lead around the Fill, I can stop in my tracks and feel wondrous delight. Like the young robins out in the world for the first time, everything seems new, unknown, and untried.

Like them, I too live in a world that is open to discovery and new possibility. And so I too am endlessly renewed.

Cinnabar Moth © Doug Parrott

18. You Kids Get Off My Lawn!

Should agents from the Bureau of Labor Statistics ever come to the Fill to take a survey about the working lives of birds, I have a feeling they would discover that June is by far their busiest month. That's because June is when most of the babies hatch and the parents say good-bye to any hope of enjoying the lazy, hazy days of summer.

Recently, for example, it was the turn of the pair of Pied-billed Grebes who have built a floating nest in the waters of Southwest Pond. For weeks, the parents have been sleeping away the days, brooding the eggs and changing places whenever that job got to be too strenuous. Occasionally, one of the adults would bring a new plant stem to add to the nest, but you could hardly call that work.

Yesterday, though, the first of four eggs hatched. I think the chick must have come out yelling—loudly. I could hear its peeps from a quarter-mile away. I hurried over to have a look and found the zebra-striped baby in a frenzy, bellowing at its parents to feed it *right now*. The parents were frantically diving for fish and stuffing their catch into the baby's mouth as fast as they could. The chick stopped peeping only long enough to swallow and then resumed its cries.

I couldn't watch, especially knowing that next summer, those poor, overwrought parents would face the same daunting challenge again. And again, year after year. I averted my eyes from the painful scene and hurried down the trail. I love children, but I have to confess I've never been that crazy about newborns, not even my own. I don't speak their language, for one thing. All that screaming and limb-flailing—what does it mean, exactly?

"Don't worry about it," said the baby nurse in the hospital, shortly after my first child was born. "Babies have different cries for different things. You'll soon know what he wants."

But I never did. He'd start turning purple, and I'd run through my laundry list of bodily essentials: change the diaper, add a blanket, delete a blanket, rock him slowly, rock him quickly, jiggle him like a can of Reddi-wip, stuff food into his open mouth. Repeat. The results were unpredictable at best, and no better when my second kid was born either. I remained clueless.

Luckily, my two colicky kids eventually outgrew their inarticulate phase and started talking. That's when I fell wholly in love with motherhood. That's also when I began to get a glimmer about how cyclical our lives are.

As a baby, it is impossible to know anything more about life than the fact that it is one way: things flow from our parents to us. When we grow up and have children ourselves, we see that the flow reverses, not to us but from us. Eventually, when we ourselves grow old and feeble, the flow reverses again.

Poets speak of this. They call it the ebb and flow of life. Or sometimes they refer to it as a circle: what goes around comes around, I guess. But as I approach the age when the magnetic poles of my life will flip again and I will enter my second childhood, I realize that the poets are only half right. Life is more of a web than a flow. We all give to each other, and we all receive, throughout our lives. Even the youngest child gives unimaginably precious gifts of love, and even the oldest of the old continue to give examples of how to face the trials of life.

My mother, bless her heart, tried to show me this at a young age. When I was seven years old, she told me and my three siblings that on May 1, we were going to distribute 70 paper baskets to the residents of the Caroline Kline Galland Home, a home for the aged in south Seattle. Most of the residents were immigrants from the Old Country, Jewish men and women who had come to America

Pied-billed Grebe chick © Doug Parrott

to escape anti-Semitism and create opportunity for their children. My mother was the secretary at the home, and she realized that May Day was a cherished but neglected holiday for these relicts of old Europe. So she went to Van Asselt, our elementary school, and enlisted our teachers in the effort to make two beautiful flower baskets for each resident. She promised that her four kids would pick enough wildflowers to fill each basket.

The teachers responded enthusiastically. Each one created a unique design and taught her students how to fold construction paper into baskets. On May 1, my mother collected the baskets, drove us to the nursing home, walked us to the wild lands that stretched from the main building all the way down to Lake Washington, and said, "Start picking."

For hours we picked everything from willow buds to magnolia blossoms, rhododendron clusters, and bluebells. By dinnertime, we had filled all the baskets with flowers. We lugged them into the building and began hanging baskets on each resident's doorknob. Our hands were raw from getting pricked by the brambles and stung by the nettles that grew among the flowers. Our faces were streaked with sweat and dust. But our baskets were stunning.

Most of the residents were in the dining room eating dinner and knew nothing about the surprise awaiting them on their return to their rooms. We kids were glad about that! We disliked the thought of getting kissed and hugged by strangers, so we hurried to finish.

Just as I was hanging my last basket on the last doorknob of the top floor, the door was jerked open and Mrs. Olswang stuck her unlovely face out of the crack.

Mrs. Olswang was the meanest, crabbiest resident in the entire home. She was so universally unpleasant, even the nurses were afraid of her. I had been terrified of her ever since the first time I met her. She had been wading in a small pond in the front yard, her skirts hitched up, her bare, stick-like legs stirring up the mud as she searched for duck eggs. "What are you looking at?" she had bellowed, when she saw me watching her. She shook her fist menacingly. "Get out of here!"

Flames shot out of her eyes, thunder rolled out of her mouth, and I could almost feel the gates of Hell opening at my feet. I fled.

Now, here she was in her lair, eyes afire, fist ready to shake. Smoke began to come out of her ears. Mutely, I held up my pathetic, handmade flower basket. Several of the wildflowers I had picked in the morning were already wilting, limp as dishrags, limp as my courage drooping under Mrs. Olswang's fearsome glare. "Happy May Day," I quavered.

Mrs. Olswang looked at the flowers. "For me?" she asked in the softest tone I had ever heard. Her wrinkled hands reached out to take the basket from me, and she wrapped her arthritic fingers around the handle. I was about to run away, relieved to be alive, when Mrs. Olswang grabbed me, hugged me to her sagging breasts, and breathed, "Thank you, child." Then she kissed my head and smiled at me.

Later that evening, I told my mom I never, ever wanted to make flower baskets again. My brothers and sister chimed in, "We don't either." We complained that it was too hard to pick all those flowers. We were embarrassed about Mom asking our teachers for help. We hated getting kissed by strangers. We had better things to do with our precious childhoods. I was still terrified by Mrs. Olswang's meanness and her even more frightening metamorphosis into something recognizably human. What could I possibly rely on in this world if even Mrs. Olswang could be nice for once?

"Well," said my mother, "I'm sorry to hear you didn't have any fun today. I'm sorry you had to give up your whole day and work so hard. But you are the only children many of these residents ever see. They're old people, they need children in their lives—everyone does—and you are elected. So get used to it because you're going to be doing it again next year." And we did.

Now I am approaching the age that Mrs. Olswang must have been all those years ago. My joints ache, and I'm sure my face often sets itself into lines of pain amid the ever-expanding wrinkles. I imagine I could easily frighten a child, if she saw me frowning as I tried to step across a big puddle at the Fill, my pants hitched up, my stick legs showing. I think about how easy it would be to let grumpiness take over, as it did the other day when I heard the shrill shouts of kids running amok along the trails. They were disturbing the peace and quiet of the Fill, throwing stones into ponds, hitting the native plants with sticks.

But just as I was about to raise my fist and shout, "You kids get out of here!" (thus imparting to them the wisdom that wildness is to be tolerated in critters but not in kids), I heard my mother's voice. "We all need children in our lives."

She meant we all need the chaos that children bring us because life is not orderly and we need to remember that. She meant we need the growth that children embody, because as they grow, so do we. She meant we need the exuberance that children have, because otherwise we would give in to the weariness that age does bring. Most of all, my mother meant we need the life force and innocent sense of wonder that children bring to the world, because when we see those qualities in them, we can call them up in ourselves as well.

Children take, but they also give. Adults give, but we also receive. We once were children like them; they will become adults like us. We help each other. I smiled, understanding my mother at last.

"Hey, you kids!" I shouted at the rampagers. "Come over here. I want to show you something." I pointed to some Purple Loosestrife flourishing in the mudflats of Main Pond. "This is an alien invader from another world. It's going to take over the Fill if we don't do something. Can you destroy it with your sticks?"

The kids began to flail. Bits of flowers, leaves, and stalks flew in every direction. After a little while, the kids' strokes grew more labored. Fighting aliens was harder than they thought, but they didn't give up. When they had reduced all the loosestrife to mere nubbins, they stopped and looked at me. Their faces were streaked with dirt, but their grins were bright.

"Next time you come," I said, "if you find any alien loosestrife, I hope you can save us again."

"We will," they shouted, and ran away.

19. Home

The two baby flickers who hatched in the snag on the banks of University Slough made their first appearance today. They poked their tufty heads out of their nest hole like Laurel and Hardy trying to exit a door at the same time. Then they cried piteously for someone to feed them. The dad soon appeared with a fresh beakful of bugs and stuffed them into the wide-open mouths.

I think I know this dad. Earlier in the year, he would station himself on the top of the light standard in the Dime Lot every morning and whang away on the metal. This is how Northern Flicker males impress females. The male who hammers the loudest is considered most desirable, I suppose because loud and persistent hammering indicates strength and good health. The males will need a lot of both. Female flickers expect their mates to carve out the current nest hole, help brood the eggs, and feed the young when they hatch. A prospective dad needs a lot of stamina to do all that, and hammering proves you've got what it takes.

Urban male flickers have discovered that if they pound on light poles or house roofs, they can make a much more impressive sound than if they whale away on natural tree trunks. So it wasn't unusual to see this particular male staked out on top of the metal pole in the parking lot. What was unusual, though, was this guy's technique. He had somehow figured out he could produce a deep, almost bass tone when he pounded on the metal plate that covered the hollow light pole itself, and he could make a higher-pitched, more clarion tone when he hit the metal covering the light fixture. For days,

Northern Flicker chicks © Doug Parrott

this Beethoven of woodpeckers would strut back and forth on top of the light standard, playing his two-toned composition. It was mesmerizing—almost, dare I say, riveting. He had no trouble attracting a mate and soon had transferred his drumming skills to the more practical task of hollowing out a nest hole.

Now, a few weeks later, as I sat on my camp stool by the snag, watching the parents come and go with their conveyor belt of bugs, I wondered if the babies had inherited their dad's abilities. Musical talent often runs in families, you know. Think of the Bachs, for example, or the Mozarts, not to mention Donny and Marie Osmond. Perhaps someday, the newly hatched flickers would create their own timpanic masterpieces. Or maybe, like many human children, they would rebel against their parents' old-school musical tastes and join a heavy metal band instead.

I started laughing at my own joke (heavy metal/metal light poles—get it?), when two women joggers happened by.

"What's so funny?" one inquired, jogging in place while she pulled the buds out of her ears.

"Oh, I was just noticing those two baby woodpeckers and the funny way they stick their heads out of their nest hole," I said, pointing. I didn't think the joggers would appreciate my metallic joke, but I figured everyone loves baby woodpeckers.

Just then, the dad showed up with more chow, causing the kids to greet him with acclaim. "That is so cute," said the jogger. "Look at how the mom takes care of her babies." She turned to her companion. "Doesn't it make you want to go home and make a nice, cozy nest for yourself, too?"

"Yes," said the second jogger. "With a cup of tea, an afghan, and a good book. That sounds lovely." They both beamed at me.

I was at a loss for words. It's one thing to mistake a male flicker for a female—really, only a bird or a birder would bother to tell them apart. But to think that a nest is a cozy home is something else. Birds' nests are about as far away from cozy as you can get. Nests are magnets for predators, parasites, and pathogens. Nest mortality reaches as high as 78 percent for some species. And it's not always outside forces that are the problem. Sometimes, the babies attack each other, as the stronger sibling tries to kill off the weaker one and grab more food for itself. It's no accident that every known bird species takes only one breeding season of a few weeks or months for the babies to fledge and leave the nest. They must grow up as fast as they can so they can leave before they get eaten or get sick and die.

In fact, birds don't really have homes—cozy or otherwise—as we understand the term. They don't own property. Instead, they *use* their environment to fulfill their needs: food, breeding, sleeping, hiding. At certain times of the year, birds may claim a portion of their habitat as territory, which they will defend against interlopers. But territories are usually temporary, established for a short while and a specific purpose. For example, birds may seek to protect a food supply or a nest. But when the food runs out or nesting is over, the birds leave.

Mammals, being less mobile than birds, tend to establish territories that are more permanent. Some even have a central base, such as a den or a cave, where they feel protected and safe. A few woodpecker species are similar, roosting in their nest holes year-round. I guess you could say this is home. But home for humans is far more than a refuge from enemies, or a place to roost.

"Home is where you fit in and feel welcome," said a gay man whom I had asked to define his idea of home. His parents had evicted him when they learned he was gay.

"Home is where you feel protected," said a foster kid who had grown up in an abusive household before she fled. "It doesn't have to be a place. It can be a person or even an idea."

"Home is where your people have always lived," said a member of the Colville Tribe, whose people were displaced by the building of the Grand Coulee Dam.

"Home is where you belong," said a refugee who had been kicked out of his country because he believed in the "wrong" religion.

"There is no place like home," said Dorothy before she clicked her heels.

"Home is where the heart is," said Pliny the Elder, a revered Roman philosopher of the first century.

"Those are all pretty good definitions," said my husband admiringly, when I asked him about his own definition of home. "Especially Pliny's."

I could see he wanted to come up with a zinger that was even better. John prides himself on thinking of punchy aphorisms that make our kids scream. He calls them bumper-sticker quotes. Beating Pliny, though—one of the greatest aphorists in history—wasn't going to be easy. John's brow wrinkled in thought. Time passed. I waited for enlightenment, but the tank seemed empty. However, you can't block a physicist for long.

"He's like a Whac-A-Mole," our oldest son once said. "You think you've got him down, but then he pops right back up again."

Sure enough, in a few minutes John said, "Home is the haven you create, where people love you, believe in you, and support you."

A bit wordy, perhaps, but I like the idea about *creating* a home. It's liberating to believe you can build whatever kind of home you want. If you come from a bad home, you can build a happy one. You don't have to replicate the unhappy one you grew up in. If you want your home to be a Superman-like Fortress of Solitude, you can feel free to make it so. If you prefer a *Cheaper by the Dozen* style, that's okay too.

The home John and I have created is a place filled with stories. Every object in it has some connection to a beloved family member or friend. Each represents a treasured memory of the past, a memory that we hope will give all who come here the strength to become whatever they want to be in the future.

We believe a home should be a place where people come to get renewed, and where we will all do everything we can to help make dreams come true. But because we are all such different people, our dreams and stories are all very different, too. This works fine when it comes to demographics—not so much when it involves decor. Style-wise, Ye Olde Curiosity Shop has nothing on us.

Sometimes I envy the homes I visit that are visions of perfection, where each objet is one d'art, where the sight lines are spare and beautiful, a home whose yards are sculpted into landscapes where no weed would dare to grow. My home, by contrast, is the one house on the block that always gets a doorknob flyer advertising yard services, typically those specializing in weed and moss removal. Evidently, the service providers think our family's focus on cultivating our psyches should be redirected to cultivating our sod.

Inside, my home reflects the same choices as our great outdoors. It is cluttered and usually dusty. None of my dishes match, and my dining room chairs have tooth marks where the cat has sharpened her teeth.

To turn my home into something *Sunset Magazine* might feature is not beyond my scope. All it would require is the commitment. In the early years of our marriage, I did try. I bought an art lamp with multiple soaring chromium arms that bend gracefully over our sofa. My husband is always hitting his head on the bulbs. He calls it

Red-eared Slider © Kathrine Lloyd

the Hydra. It uses special lightbulbs that are almost impossible to find anymore. Only one lightbulb currently works. When that one burns out, I'm not sure what I'll do. I did suggest the other day that I should take the lamp down to the Goodwill and donate it. "You can't get rid of the Hydra!!" everyone cried, horrified.

People in my family make the same outcry whenever I suggest getting rid of any of the other bazillion things that fill my home to overflowing. I guess it's because to my family, each object in our house represents the overflowing of love, of history and stories. That is home to them, and they don't want it to ever change.

Back at the woodpecker snag a few days later—where life is simple and the clutter is confined to the occasional beer can left behind by the college kids—I checked on the two babies. Their feathers looked more adult. It won't be long now before they leave their hole to fly free, as all woodpeckers eventually must. I set down my camp stool to watch the parents come by with more food. It's always relaxing to watch someone else do the chores. The Sun shone through the Lombardy Poplars lining the slough, and a little breeze ruffled the water, making reflections shimmer up the gnarled wood of the snag. A turtle slowly climbed up out of the water and onto a log, a little mud still clinging to its carapace. I remembered another definition of home, this one by Kirkpatrick Sale in his book, *Christopher Columbus and the Conquest of Paradise*: "The Spanish have a word, 'querencia,' which implies not merely a 'love of home' as the dictionaries say, but a deep, quiet sense of inner well-being that comes from knowing a particular place of the earth, its diurnal and seasonal patterns, its fruits and scents, its history and its part in your history. It is that place where, whenever you return to it, your soul releases an inner sigh of recognition and relaxation."

I took a deep breath and let it out slowly in perfect contentment. I am home.

20. Extra Ordinary

From the very beginning of my birding passion, I have loved the new birds, the ones I have never seen before. Partly, I love them because each new species is testimony to the diversity of life on our planet and to the long process of evolution that, protein by protein, created each life form unique from every other that ever existed. Partly, I love the fact that a new species stimulates a new quest for knowledge, as I seek to understand this bird's life and the journey that brought it here. Partly, it's because I love lists, and a new bird means a new addition to my life list.

When our family began birding, we had a rule that in order to add a new bird to our life list, every member of the family had to see it. Each weekend, I would look at my watch at some point and announce, "Time to go down to Montlake Fill and find a new bird." We would all pile into the car and go for an outing, a treasure hunt, an adventure.

In those days, every bird was new to us, even a Mallard. Of course, we had seen Mallards many times in the past, so they weren't precisely a brand-new bird. The kids and I had often fed them bread before we learned we weren't supposed to do that. I learned this the hard way when I took the baby to the park one day to throw bread to the ducks. Alex was nine months old. He couldn't throw the bread very far, so gradually, the ducks gathered around us. One of the Mallards was especially aggressive. He kept waddling closer so he could grab every piece before the other ducks could. Eventually, we ran out of bread; unfortunately, this happened before the Mallard ran out of appetite. The duck simply would not accept the fact that we had nothing more to feed him. He began to hiss in frustration, and when this did not produce the desired result, he came at us with his bill snapping. I whirled the baby stroller around and took off for the parking lot, duck in hot pursuit. My stroller wasn't designed for cross-country races. Instead of the molded polymer wheels outfitted with pneumatic tires that real racing strollers have, my stroller had little plastic wheels the size of tea saucers. You wouldn't think a person could get much speed from a vehicle like that, but you'd be amazed what you can do when an angry duck is after you.

No, Mallards were not new to our family. But they became new when we took up birding. That's because when you're birding, you must look at all the field marks of any given bird. You've got to take note of plumage variations, overall shape of bird, its size, behavior, sounds, habitat. You see a bird in ways you never did before, and thus it becomes new.

Mallard © Doug Parrott

For a year, we kept adding new birds to our life list simply by walking around the Fill. Eventually, we began to see more of the usual suspects and fewer of the exciting newbies. The adventure started to pall. Birding was in danger of becoming more drudgery than delight. I consulted my friend Pat Hitchens, a wonderful birder and mentor. Pat had more than 600 birds on her life list. "If you want to see new species," she said, "you have to go to new habitat."

Thus began our odysseys. Every chance we got, we tried to get out into new habitat. Because of birding, we visited the mountains and the shore. We explored old growth forests and the shrub-steppe of the drylands. We drove to southeast Arizona and came back past the Great Salt Lake of Utah. We visited relatives in the Midwest and birded along the way. We went hiking, camping, cycling, canoeing. We swam with otters in icy mountain lakes and ate wild blueberries in company with bears.

It was all great fun for us, but for me, the greatest draw was always the birds. One day, I realized the rest of my family might not be quite as enthralled with birds as I was. We were on a pelagic birding trip out of Westport, on a day when the seas were very rough. My youngest son became violently seasick, so we gave him a Dramamine and laid him on a bench to sleep. All was fine until suddenly, a Sabine's Gull hove into view. It was a glorious bird, its dramatic black, gray, and white wings catching the wind off the face of enormous swells, its yellow-tipped bill gleaming like gold in the sparkling sunshine. The gull was one of the most beautiful birds I had ever seen, but it wasn't going to count on our life list because Nathan was fast asleep on a bench. Thinking quickly, I ran to the bench, snatched up my sleeping child, aimed his face at the gull, and yelled, "Nathan, open your eyes!!"

Groggily, Nathan squinted at the water. "Uh, uh, uh," he said, confused by the madwoman yelling at him to look at the bird, look at the bird. The gull disappeared over the horizon, Nathan's head sank onto my shoulder as he went back to sleep, and I realized I had gone around the bend. Luckily, my son has no memory of this event, so my guilt has faded over the years.

That was the last time we birded as a family. We still go on adventures, but they are not birding adventures. For years after my episode, I chased new species alone or with just my husband. My longest chase was to Siberia to look for Steller's Sea Eagles. My nuttiest chase was to Martha's Vineyard the day after I heard a Red-footed Falcon had shown up there, the first one ever seen in North America. As my life list grew long, my budget grew short. When I could no longer justify the expense, I went back to my mentor Pat and asked her what I should do.

"Find something else you like about birds besides new species," she said. "I found painting." Pat is a renowned artist who is inspired by the elegant serenity of nature. She has a special affinity for birds, of course—she combines her deep knowledge of birds with her artistic talent to produce compelling paintings that reveal the inner beauty of the wild.

I nodded my head in understanding, but while my chin was pistoning up and down, my brain was stuck in neutral. What else could possibly be as much fun as adding new species to my life list? I went down to the Fill to cogitate. As I sat beside Main Pond, a pair of Mallard males paddled near. Mallard males are done breeding now that it's summer and the females have taken over the task of raising the young. This gives the males a chance to shed their conspicuous breeding feathers and change into plumage that camouflages them better. This pair was still pretty brightly colored, but they won't be much longer. Soon they will look as drab as any female.

The duck closest to shore was eyeing a tasty plant near my camp stool. I could see the debate going on in his head: Was the risk of coming near me worth the reward? His pal, a far more conservative fellow, hung back. Keeping a wary eye on me, the male waddled out of the water and began nibbling the plant. He was so close, I could hear the little clicks his bill made as he tore off bites.

For a moment, I was pulled back in time to the day I sat with my uncle in his kitchen in South Bend. I was sixteen. He had made a stew and was slurping his portion with a spoon. My uncle's English wasn't perfect. Even after many years in this country, he still had a heavy accent. "Eat, eat," he said. "It's good zuppa." His dentures clicked as he smacked his lips.

It was the exact sound the Mallard made as he chomped a beakful of plants. Emily Post, the maven of manners, would have been appalled by the duck's homely eating habits, but I realized if I wanted to continue watching him at my feet, I would have to keep quiet, just as I had never breathed a word of criticism to my uncle. Neither the duck nor my uncle were aware of breaking Emily's rigid rules of etiquette, and they would have been baffled to be told they were. Life for them was all about gusto, not grace. I was utterly charmed.

The timid Mallard soon joined his companion, and his dentures began to click, too. Now the chatter sounded like a couple pairs of false teeth that you wind up at a joke shop. I couldn't help myself. I laughed out loud. Fortunately, the ducks didn't take offense, and so we enjoyed brunch together.

It was the first of many such times that birds reminded me of people I know, and all so humorously.

I still love to see new birds. When a rarity appears at the Fill, I can feel my whole soul light up, as though the Sun itself was burning within me. But it is moments like the ones the Mallards shared that I have come to love even more. They made me realize how wonderful it is to treasure the everyday joys of ordinary life. Transcendent moments that make my spirit soar come few and far between. They are, I must admit, the essence of fun. But I cannot rely on such rarities to make me happy, for they come too seldom and pass too quickly. To create more lasting happiness, I must seek the little joys that may be small but are everywhere at hand. All I have to do to access them is stop, savor the moment, and realize at the conscious level how happy I am right then.

There are countless opportunities to do this, both at the Fill and anywhere else I go, or even if I go nowhere at all. I can thus experience happiness hundreds of times a day.

Having fun is great. Being happy is greater. There is a difference.

21. Black Magic

I suppose someday, in our steady march toward constructing the Theory of Everything, we will know all there is to know about the lives of Black Swifts, one of the most secretive and least understood birds in all the world. But that day is not yet.

Black Swifts are scimitar-shaped flyers who spend most of their lives in South America—no one knows just where. They arrive here in June on their way to nesting sites behind waterfalls in the Cascades—no one knows exactly which ones or how many. Behind the torrents of falling water, the swifts raise their young—no one knows precisely how.

In the early mornings of the summer, when storm clouds gather over the foothills to the east, the swifts leave their mountain fasts and wing their way to us down here in the lowlands. They come to hunt insects on the fly, soaring so quickly overhead they can appear out of nowhere and vanish if you blink your eyes. Like magic.

So mysterious and enchanting are these Black Swifts that they might well be the stuff of fairy tales, perhaps even tales like this one:

Once upon a time, there was a king of the Western Mountains whose secret castle lay behind a waterfall. None knew how to find the castle except the king himself. To keep the secret, he would wait until the sun was just about to rise in the early morning and the moon was just beginning to set behind the peaks of his home. In the dim light of the dawn, he would stand on the edge of the parapet, spread out his arms, and recite an incantation. As the magic words poured from his lips, his skin grew dark and feathery, his

Black Swifts at a waterfall © Glen Tepke

arms transformed into wings, and his flowing cloak became a forked tail. Then he would burst forth from the waterfall and fly down to the farms and valleys of his kingdom far below, where he would hunt all day long, flitting here and there, appearing but briefly to his entranced subjects.

At dusk, he would hurry back to his watery gateway, make sure no one was watching, then dart swiftly through the cascading falls and into his home. There, he would shake off the glistening drops of water from his shoulders, recite another spell to become human again, and think about the happy day of hunting he had had.

But one day the king grew sad. He had no wife to live in his castle, no children to praise his hunting or laugh at his stories, no one with whom to share the glories of the wind. He spoke to his friend, the Cliff Swallow, who came north each summer to build a mud nest under the eaves of a house in the valley. The king's friend never seemed to have any trouble finding a girl to share his nest, and each year, he and his mate raised three or four kids.

"Are you nuts?" said his friend, when he learned the king was thinking of marriage. "You want to give up your man-castle and let some female take it over? She'll tell you it's messy, and you'll have to clean it up every weekend. She'll say you're hunting too much and need to spend more time with her. She'll decide you've got to talk about feelings. And that's just the start. Wait till the kids arrive! You'll be taking out fecal sacs round the clock. You'll be run ragged trying to feed bottomless pits. And when they finally leave the nest, they'll pester you with demands to keep them in bugs, even after they're perfectly able to find their own."

The king listened very carefully to his friend's tirade, but he noticed one thing his friend did not say. Despite all his gripes, his friend never said he was lonely or bored. "What he has is what I want, too," the king said to himself. And so he began to search for the girl of his dreams.

He started by making a list. "She must be adventurous," he thought, "because it won't be easy to change from girl to bird and back every day. She's got to love travel, because I migrate a long way every year. She should be kind and generous, and she's got to love me for myself, not because I'm a king and happen to own a castle."

The king searched far and wide for his true love, but nowhere could he find a girl to share his life. Lots of women were attracted by the idea of marrying a king, but when they found out his castle was really a cavern behind a cold, dank waterfall, they lost interest. Plus, they weren't too crazy about having to flap their way to and from a distant land twice a year. And the insect diet was right out.

But the king would not give up. Day after day, he flew high above the farms of his kingdom, looking for the right girl to love. One day, he was soaring as high as a king can soar, when all of a sudden a Boeing 787 Dreamliner flew past him. Its powerful turbojets roiled the air, caught up the king, and threw him this way and that, tearing his feathers. The wind beat against him, until he lost his senses and plunged down, falling, falling all the long way to the ground. He hit with a sickening thump and lay still.

Toward evening, the reapers left their fields and turned homeward, to a warm hearth and a hot meal waiting. The fields were left empty, except for the poor gleaners, who were allowed to comb through the wheat stalks looking for a few kernels of grain left behind. One such gleaner was a young girl with sharp eyes and a kind heart. As she stooped over the ground, looking for food, she saw a raggedy bundle of black feathers. Thinking it was a starling she might be able to bring home for the cooking pot, she carefully picked it up, only to discover it was a Black Swift, a bird known to her only from brief glimpses in the sky. "Oh," she breathed in wonder, and softly touched her lips to the limp form.

Naturally, her kiss revived the king, who looked up into the gentlest, most beautiful eyes he had ever seen and promptly lost his heart. It was love at first sight. Without thinking, he transformed himself into a man so he could ask his newfound love to marry him. This jolt would have given most girls a heart attack, but the gleaner girl was made of sterner stuff, and she took it all without a blink. Well, maybe her eyes bugged out a little. However, the newly transformed young man standing before her was very handsome, and although she had always loved the high-flying swifts, she liked him even more.

Blushing a little at her own daring, she smiled at him, took the hand he offered, and fell in love herself. And so they were wed. After the honeymoon was over, the king taught his beloved queen how to transform herself into a swift too, and forevermore they soared through life together.

The End.

Magic has a bad name these days. We say it is merely illusion, or primitive ignorance, or childish belief in the supernatural. Science has taught us there is no monster under the bed, no voodoo that can make your unpleasant boss feel like she's being poked with pins, no matter how many you stick into her doll. Science has explained to us how the Sun appears to rise in the east and set in the west, day after day, without any ceremonies or sacrifices from us. Science tells us how and when the rain will come, how disease can kill or be cured. Science invented cell phones and explains how they work, though they still seem magical to me.

Science has yet to figure out why my husband's imitation of Dr. Strangelove is so funny, but it's only a matter of time until science has distilled every thought and feeling into mere chemistry. Bit by bit, science is driving out magic, and I guess that's a good thing.

But I hope science never drives out wonder. When a Black Swift floats in midair a few feet above my head, as one did earlier this week, his button-black eyes staring into mine for a brief moment while he spreads out his wings and his little forked tail to hover over me, he is wonderful. My heart floats away with him, and I am wonder full, as well.

Cliff Swallow feeding young © Tim Kuhn

22. Oxygen

The two Marsh Wrens who lay claim to the cattails of Southeast Pond have been venturing forth into unknown territory recently. It all started when they ratcheted themselves up the little tree that grows amid the cattails on the north end of the pond. From there, they could look over a vast spread of prairie, where sparrows and finches have been feasting on the grass seeds and chicory that grow here so abundantly.

Something about the prairie or the other birds must have attracted the wrens, because, after venturing up the tree each morning for a few days, they finally mustered the courage to fly over the Loop Trail that separates the pond from the field, crossing the Rubicon, as it were. Since then, they have roamed all over the field. I hear them chittering among the grass tufts that rise from the prairie like miniature teepees on the Great Plains. If the air is still, I can follow their progress by the twitching of the grass tufts.

Occasionally, one of the wrens will pop out on top of a grass stem to see what's what before diving back into the greensward. The marsh that figures so largely in their names seems a distant memory to them, at least for now. "Marsh?" they seem to say. "What are you talking about?"

It's a reminder that although we humans like to give names to everything, thereby categorizing and locking all living beings into niches, the ones thusly named do not have to agree to stay put. Marsh Wrens can be prairie wrens whenever they want. And who knows? Maybe they'll become forest wrens someday, or mountain wrens, or Lexus-driving suburban wrens. Whatever they do, it won't be up to human agency to set their internal limits. It never was.

Maybe the reason I love the essential wildness of wrens—their intractable resistance to total control by us—is that I like to think that I too am free from the control of "us." Not that I think I am above the laws that govern society. On the contrary, when the street sign on the corner says, "No turn on red," I always wait for the light to turn green. Heck, I am even one of those nutty but nice Seattleites you'll find standing on a deserted corner in the dark and the rain, with no cars in sight, waiting for the pedestrian light to say I can walk across the street. I do it because I believe in the rule of law, and I also admit there is a certain element that directs me to bow to the power of social pressure to conform.

But that is where I want to draw a line in the sand, a line that says, "On this side, you agree to be bound, but otherwise you are free." I'm happy to conform to commonsensical laws and rules that make civil society possible. In return, I want the autonomy to define my own version of the good life and pursue my own vision of happiness without society having the authority to dictate who I am or what I can become. In other words, I want freedom of mind and spirit.

It is true that nature does not grant such freedom to its wildlife. None of the plants and animals in nature have untrammeled free will. They are governed by instinct and environment, a simple fact that limits their choices. But plants and animals cannot build their own environment, as we so ubiquitously do. Creating our own environment—both physical and social—gives us much more leeway to make our own choices, whether as a society or as an individual. Much as I am embedded in my own culture, I choose to reject the limits that other people place on my inner life. There, I truly want to be as free of human constraint as the Marsh Wrens are.

One way I can do this is to make the best of whatever situation I am in. "Making the best of it" has devolved in our culture. It used to be a phrase of commendation: Anybody who made the best of something had found a way to spin straw into gold. That ability was admired in the days when most people were farmers and had

Marsh Wren © Doug Parrott

a lot more straw than gold. Nowadays, nobody wants to make the best of anything because the phrase has come to mean settling for something much less than the best. And why would anyone want to do that? It sounds a lot like giving up.

But I think we have failed to understand the essential word in the phrase. That word is not "best" (translation: second-best). It is "making." Making implies that we can take raw materials and create something new, something useful and good.

The philosopher Ludwig Wittgenstein called it making his own oxygen. Wittgenstein was a celebrated professor at the University of Cambridge. One day, he was approached by one of his students, who had been thinking of leaving school. Wittgenstein told him it was a good idea. "It is essential that you get away from Cambridge at once," he said. "There is no oxygen for you at Cambridge."

Given that Wittgenstein himself was a full professor at the school, perhaps the student can be forgiven for looking askance at this statement. What about the old English saying, "What's good for the goose is good for the gander?"

"Oh," said Wittgenstein, "it doesn't matter for me, as I manufacture my own oxygen."

To manufacture our own oxygen, we must *actively* search for the innate properties in every situation that offer us the opportunity to create fulfillment. Nearly every environment has within it some feature that gives us a chance to grow—or the choice to shrink. If we can identify anything in that feature that we can perceive as a positive force, we can use it to grow from within.

For example, my environment of Egyptology at the University of Chicago became untenable when recession hit in the 1970s and my department could no longer afford to support its doctoral and postdoctoral students. Like any bird without enough sustenance, I had to leave. It was a painful decision. I had wanted to be an Egyptologist since the age of four.

I looked for a job that might be as engaging as Egyptology had always been for me and found that the *Bulletin of the Atomic Scientists* needed an editor. I knew nothing about physics, atomic or otherwise, but I knew a lot about language. I applied. The managing editor who interviewed me said, "Hm, Egyptologist. You must like details. You're hired."

On my first day of work, she told me regretfully that my job had disappeared. It turned out that Anne, the production manager, had wanted to switch to editorial and thought it was unfair for the magazine to hire an outsider. "So I gave Anne your job," said the managing editor.

"What am I supposed to do?" I asked, bewildered by this switch.

"Oh, you can have Anne's job," the managing editor airily said. "We'll train you."

I hadn't even known there was such a job as magazine production, but I needed to eat, so I agreed. Thus began a 30-year career in print production. I learned how to set type, manage four-color separations, paste up galleys, and direct pressmen to reproduce color accurately. I met wonderful craftsmen along the way who generously helped me learn as much as I could absorb. I traveled to exotic places to oversee printing. I developed a passion for the craft, a passion I still feel to this day.

Gradually, I began to write for the magazines I produced. Magazines always need little pieces to fill in blank spaces—book reports, equipment reviews, event announcements. I discovered that writing was my true calling and eventually became a freelance writer. Now I am an author.

Recently, I realized that my dream to become an Egyptologist was not the dream I had always believed it was. I had never been interested in digging up artifacts. It was the culture that had always fascinated me, and even more, it was the desire to teach others about an ancient people who were very like us. I wanted to tell their stories so others would feel as connected to the past—and to the great panoply of cultures that we humans have invented—as I did. In other words, what I really wanted to be all my life was a writer. I just didn't recognize it until I was forced to find something engaging about magazine production, something that would turn it into an abiding passion.

My passion for magazine production was noticed by my bosses, who sought to give me an opportunity to grow artistically in whatever direction I wanted. Passion became art, and art became my opportunity to create. This all happened because I *made* the best of my situation.

Marsh Wrens make the best of it, too. I don't know how consciously they do so—maybe their brains only react biochemically to stimuli. On the other hand, science is telling me that maybe that's all my brain does, too. Since I utterly reject this conclusion, it makes no difference to me why the Marsh Wrens make the best of it. The fact that they do is just another reason I like them so much.

At the Fill, Marsh Wrens usually weave their covered nests among the cattails that line the waters of Union Bay. The marshes here are the biggest on all of Lake Washington and host several breeding pairs of wrens. Recently, though, the wren population has exploded to the point where all the best cattails have been claimed.

Marsh Wren building a nest near Canal Road © Doug Parrott

Young wrens starting their first families have either had to leave or accept marginal territories.

One male who decided to make the best of it earlier this summer built his nest among the woody branches of scrub willows that grow along the grubby ditch below the baseball diamond along Canal Road. The nest was at head height out in the open, so it was uncharacteristically easy to see. Several of us birders watched the little guy fetch cattail leaves and weave them into a beautiful nest. When he was done, we applauded his workmanship. He had built something from nothing, and it was a beautiful job.

His mate disagreed. She had him build several other nests so she could choose the best one. Marsh Wren females have been doing this for eons, and I guess the males are used to it by now. In the end, she chose a nest among the cattails of University Slough across the road. The male must have shrugged his figurative shoulders and buckled down to help raise the young.

When your motto is, "Make the best of it," you find a way to get with the program and be happy, no matter what your mate or fate in general might throw at you, creating a life that is beautiful and good.

Or, as Martin Luther King, Jr., put it, "When our days become dreary with low-hovering clouds of despair, and when our nights become darker than a thousand midnights, let us remember that there is a creative force in this universe, working to pull down the gigantic mountains of evil, a power that is able to make a way out of no way and transform dark yesterdays into bright tomorrows."

Changing the world, as Martin Luther King did, is far beyond my pay grade. I'm more at the wren level. There, out in nature, I observe the wrens working hard every year to create bright tomorrows. And I know that I can, too.

23. Can You Hear Me Now?

I ran into a birder the other day who was standing near Kern's Restoration Pond, looking frustrated. "What's up?" I asked, prepared for a dog-off-its-leash story, or something similar.

"I can hear a Common Yellowthroat in there singing, but darned if I can find him," complained the birder.

I know the feeling. Common Yellowthroat males are among the most beautiful of all our summer warblers. They have sun-bright yellow fronts and a dramatic black mask across their eyes. Imagine a combination of Liberace and Zorro, only downsized to something not much bigger than a golf ball, and you'll get the picture.

You'd think a Common Yellowthroat would be easy to see in this getup, but the opposite is true. A male can sing literally inches away and yet remain completely hidden. When he finally does move, you realize you've been staring in the correct vicinity but have somehow missed the bird.

"Well," I said, trying to console the birder, "we're not dolphins, you know. We can't echolocate," and I gave a little ping.

The birder gave me "the Look" and then harrumphed off. Reflecting on the fact that I had always previously thought only women were capable of executing the Look, I sat down on my camp stool and prepared to wait for the yellowthroat to sing again. Shortly, he did but remained hidden. I scanned the habitat. The bird appeared to be in a patch of leafy bushes that couldn't have been larger than a bathtub, but it was simply impossible to find him.

Then I remembered owls. Owls can't echolocate like dophins either—by pinging sound off an object—but they *can* locate prey by sound. They can do it because their ears are asymmetrically positioned on their heads. One ear is higher than the other, enabling owls to tell where a scuttling mouse is, based on differences in the intensity of sound reaching each ear.

How hard can that be? I wondered. I cupped one hand behind my left ear and tilted my head to the right, maximizing the sound differential. The warbler warbled, and I strained to tell apart the intensities of sound coming to my enhanced ear versus my unadorned ear. I bent my head even further so my cupped ear was pointing almost straight up. "Do that again, you little varmint," I said, just as a jogger ran past.

"What did you call me?" she asked, giving me a different kind of Look. Then she backed up, keeping me always in view. When she had backtracked out of sight around the bend in the trail, she must have figured it was safe to turn around and run off—I could hear her feet churn the gravel on the path as she passed from my life.

Meanwhile, a flash of yellow informed me the Common Yellowthroat had also passed from my life. "Thanks a lot for making me seem weird," I told his departing form, and so to home. Once again, the Bird Lady had added a loose screw to her collection.

Socrates always said in order to be wise, "Know yourself." After years of vainly trying to fit in with other members of my species, perhaps it's a sign of wisdom to admit I live on the far end of the bell curve. For one thing, I dress funny. In the summer, I wear a mesh bug shirt so the mosquitoes that breed abundantly in the marshes and swamps of the Fill can't bite my arms while I sit on my camp stool waiting for yellowthroats to show themselves. In this outfit, I look like a walking butterfly net, topped by the distinctive floppy hat I always wear so the birds will recognize me and let me get close.

Clothes aren't my only diagnostic field mark. My behavior is far from normal, as well. I interrupt conversations to point out a bird that just passed by. I stop joggers to ask them if I can use their cell phones to report a rarity. Sometimes I ask them to carry messages to other birders who are further along on the Loop Trail. I do this when I spot a bird I know the other birders have missed. The joggers

Common Yellowthroat © Thomas Sanders

are usually happy to oblige. They are kindly people and don't mind running around the Loop Trail to look for peripatetic birders. The Sapa Inca had his runners, and I have mine.

My brain chemistry is equally idiosyncratic. I can tell you the names of hundreds of bird species but can't remember the name of that stupid plant that looks just like Queen Anne's Lace but my horticultural friend Amy says is in an entirely different family, and native. Vetch? Dock? Wild Carrot? Cyprus? No, that's an island.

Despite these quirks, or maybe because of them, I have become a known figure at the Fill. When the joggers wheeze by for the third time, circling the Loop Trail every four minutes while I advance four meters, they smile and say hello. I don't know their names, but I know them. The dog walkers who keep their dogs leashed stop to chat while I ruffle their friends' ears; the dog walkers who let their dogs run free usually head the other way if they spot me. They can tell even from a distance that my gimlet eyes are giving them the Look. Students stop a while by my camp stool to tell me about their latest courses and the big plans they have for the future. Professors describe their research. Birders who come to the Fill have become good friends.

All are as familiar to me as the birds I find here every day. We are a community, you see. We have different interests, different reasons for coming to the Fill, but despite our differences, we get along. We respect each other. In fact, the Fill succeeds on many levels—as a natural area, an open space, research facility, and bird sanctuary—because we do respect each other and this place.

It's a great feeling to be part of a flock of such disparate beings. It reminds me of the community my mother lived in as a girl. Her family emigrated from Hungary and settled in South Bend, Indiana, along with other working-class Hungarians who were drawn to the city because of job opportunities in factories. It was a tight community filled with colorful characters. One such was Mrs. Karpaty, who was told by her doctor that her lumbago would improve if she applied heat, so every sunny afternoon, she would stick her bare rump out of her second-floor window. Or Mr. Mutafan, whose wild mushrooms my mother enjoyed eating until she learned one day that Mr. Mutafan was legally blind and couldn't see the difference between a fungus and a french fry, much less between an edible mushroom and a poisonous one. Or Mrs. Horvat, who would go to the second-hand clothing store, buy the largest dress she could find, and cut out the cloth to make dresses for her three daughters. Each dress was a different style, but the girls all looked alike because the pattern of their dress fabric was the same.

Like people in any other community, my mother's neighbors bickered with each other and gossiped. Many of their disputes were carried out in full public view, with volume set high. My mom always knew when a husband and wife weren't getting along, or when a child brought home a bad report card. But as rough and raucous as people were to each other, they clung together too. At the deepest level, they accepted one another and knew they were all in this world together.

The world they inhabited was surging with new ideas, both because of the times and the place. It was the early 20th century, and people were mixing together as never before, especially in immigrant nations such as ours. People came here from all over the world, bringing their outlandish cultures with them, prepared to build new lives in strange places. It was a potent mix of old and new, a rich stew of possibility, mostly centered in our cities.

Cities have always served this purpose, ever since they were invented some 11,000 years ago in the Middle East. Cities brought people together, forcing them to learn new lessons about how to get along with each other. More important, cities allowed people from many different backgrounds to exchange ideas, synergize their creativity, and accelerate the evolution of culture. Well, when you consider that the earliest stone tools appeared in our history around 2.5 million years ago—before Homos were even sapiens—and hardly changed until about 12,000 years ago, you can see how the pace of technology has picked up. In my lifetime, we have advanced from simple piston-driven cars to spacecraft that can reach outside our own solar system. We've invented whole new food groups—

frozen pizza comes to mind—and installed computers into nearly everything, including my oven.

One unexpected benefit of the digitization of nearly everything is that today, our sense of community has expanded, as people establish virtual societies via social networks. Such societies span the globe, bringing people together in ways that were never possible before. If you have any kind of interest, no matter how specialized, you can find like-minded people somewhere in the virtual world who share that interest and who can give you new ideas to think about.

It is true that there is risk associated with these new social networks. To my mind, one of the biggest risks is that if I find many people who think just like I do, I will become too comfortable. It is fun to communicate with people who agree with us, isn't it? But we need to be confronted by people who disagree with us, who challenge our complacency, who bring totally different views to the discussion table and who delight in prodding us to get out of our comfort zone.

I doubt I will ever understand the joggers whose favorite thing to do at the Fill is sweat as they huff and puff their painful way around the Loop Trail. But I am very happy to encounter them. They give me many things to think about, including the idea that our species does best when it happily allows people to be different.

The Common Yellowthroats I hear so often at the Fill (and see so seldom!) are all pretty much the same. They all sing the same songs, wear the same colored feathers, eat the same kinds of bugs, come to the Fill about the same time and leave in the fall. They are beautiful beyond description, but they will never tell a story. Or invent a frozen pizza. Only we quirky humans—individuals all, but equally all a part of community—can do that.

24. Perfection

In the early morning of the summer, before the Sun climbs high, the stillness of the night air lingers into the day. No leaf stirs, not even the wiggly leaves of the cottonwood trees that are tied so loosely to their branches that they swivel at the slightest breath of a breeze.

On such mornings, I hurry down to Main Pond to set up my camp stool and wait for the Barn Swallows to come for their morning drink of water. Barn Swallows like to do everything on the fly, and drinking is no exception. By the dozen, they swarm down to Main Pond from their nests under the eaves of the old crew house to the south. Each swallow files its own flight plan, and then they swoop over the water in all directions, never colliding. As each bird nears the surface, it dips its head to skim a few droplets of water with its bill. The mirror of the water becomes etched with a perfect vee when the swallow finishes its drink and lifts itself back into the sky.

But that is not all the bird leaves behind. As each swallow swoops low over the water, the wind from its wings presses ripples into the smooth, shining pond. The ripples spread out a short distance and then disappear, too fine to last for long, too beautiful to stay for long, too magical for me ever to forget.

In the stillness, in the solitude, with only these wild creatures and me moving on the stage of life, it is like watching a kabuki play. Perfection.

Then a mosquito lands on my wrist and begins to drill. I realize two others have already done their work on my leg, and I begin to itch. The county guys who are spraying the shoreline to kill Yellow

Garden Loosestrife, an invasive flower, roar across the bay in their airboat. I wonder what will happen to my lungs when the pesticide blows my way. My feet hurt, my knees ache. I've been sitting on my camp stool so long my rear end has gone to sleep. I look back at Main Pond and notice that all the swallows have disappeared into the ether. My little bubble of perfection has burst, and I am back in the real world.

Or am I? Is reality always so imperfect, so noisy and itchy? Or, to put it another way, would my derriere go to sleep in paradise? And if it did, would it still *be* paradise?

Aristotle answered questions like these by saying it's all in how you define terms. He defined perfection as completion, and said a thing is complete (and perfect) if it meets three conditions: It possesses all of its requisite parts; it's so wonderful there is nothing of its kind that is superior; it has completed its purpose well and reached a good end.

You can see what a great measuring stick Aristotle's definition of perfection is. Take my Honda Insight, for example, the only car I ever loved. I bought it in the year 2000 because my youngest son and my husband both took one look at it on the car lot, and the love-light came into their eyes.

It was a silver teardrop of a car, built low and elliptical, the most efficient gas-fueled car ever rated by the EPA. The Insight was the kind of car Gort would have driven, if he had elected to stay here on Earth. (Gort, you may recall, was the silvery Art Deco robot in the 1951 sci fi flick, *The Day the Earth Stood Still.*)

My Honda Insight met all of Aristotle's perfection criteria. It possessed all its requisite parts, and, for that matter, not one part in excess. It was so wonderful, there never has been any car superior, at least to me. It completed its purpose well, namely, getting me where I wanted to go, and it did so with consummate style. Young men used to leer at me (or more accurately, my car) at stoplights, an experience unique in my existence. As for reaching a good end, I guess you could say it did that too, at least as far as I'm concerned. You see, I no longer own that incredible car. My son drove off with it when he went to college, leaving me to wave goodbye to two of my most beloveds.

Years later, my son still has that car. Parts of it have fallen off from time to time, other parts are stuck on with duct tape, still others stick when they're not supposed to. Is it still perfect? I'm not sure how to answer that question. The car still works, and thus it must have all its requisite parts. It still takes people where they want to go, and that is definitely a wonder. The car shows its age, but does that diminish its essence, its perfection? My son loves that car, and should I ever get it back into my hands, I would too. It satisfies me in ways I cannot articulate.

Brazilian artist Jane Sandes might very well understand. She is a highly respected painter and sculptor who lives in Fortaleza. I asked her how an artist of her caliber defines perfection. "When I am painting," she answered, "the creative process only ends after I achieve what I view as perfection. If I am happy with the result, and if the result satisfies me, then I'll stop working on the piece. Artists do not and should not rely on someone else to approve their work; an artist should produce art to satisfy him or herself only. As such, I believe that artists should commit to themselves before committing to an audience."

I like Sandes's focus on an inner definition of perfection. Too often, we allow other people to define what is acceptable in our lives. They tell us whether we are beautiful or ugly, fat or thin, smart or stupid, lovable, worthy, valuable—or not. Often, it is their negative voices that get installed in our heads, so even when they themselves are long gone, we hear them still telling us how inadequate we are, how far from perfection, how impossible it is for us ever to reach the heights. If we listen to those voices, we will never need a bully to beat us up—we do such a good job of that ourselves.

Then why listen? Why not, instead, be the best you can, do the best you can, and let go of the rest? Will you be perfect? No. But as Aristotle said, the word "perfect" means complete and finished. Are you ever finished? Do you want to be? Or do you want to continue to evolve and change?

Sitting beside Main Pond, scratching my mosquito bites, I looked at the dead willow snag that keeps its woody feet wedged deep in the mud, refusing to let loose. Years ago, it was a vigorous tree with flowing leaves that caressed the water in summer. But Main Pond has grown larger over time as the land continues to sink under the weight of the garbage that presses down upon it. Willow trees cannot survive if their roots are always wet, and eventually this one died.

Now it serves as a perch for the Barn Swallows who preen on its branches after they have drunk their fill. It shades the mud gathered at its base, providing cover for the Virginia Rails who raise their chicks here every year. It gives food to the woodpeckers who come here in the early morning to listen for insects inside the wood.

Two years ago, the snag blew over and cracked. Yet still it holds on. I suppose eventually its roots will weaken and it will fall completely into the water and rot away, giving its nutrients back to the pond. I will not rue that day because I know that new life will grow where the old snag stands.

Main Pond was an Eden when the willow was young and vigorous. It is an Eden now that the tree is dead but still useful. It will be an Eden in the future when the tree is only a memory. The Fill is never finished, you see. But it is always perfectly beautiful. Perfection, in my eyes, is not flawless. It is free.

Barn Swallow © Doug Parrott

25. Treasure

Once upon a time, a powerful mage was asked by the king to create a marvel. The king was giving a soirée for the royals living one kingdom down the road, and he wanted to impress his guests with his own potency. He figured any king who had a mage at his beck and call was a pretty powerful guy.

Caught off guard at the very moment he was eating a puff pastry, the mage swallowed quickly and tried to think of something marvelous. But all he could think of was how irritating it was to work for a guy who wouldn't even give you a decent lunch break. So waving his magic wand, the mage created a great pile of greenbacks in the middle of the dining room.

The king and his guests all fell silent, staring at the small bits of green paper stacked in neat bricks of one hundred to the stack. "Er, what is it?" asked the bewildered king.

"It is money," said the mage, and took another pastry.

For many years after that, people puzzled about what to do with money. They didn't quite know what it was good for. But slowly, over time, they began to understand.

"Money," said the farmer, "is a convenience. Now when I want to buy some shoes for my children, I don't have to haul a barrel of milk over to the shoemaker's shop. I just take my wallet."

"Money," said the CEO, smiling at the farmer's naïveté, "is power. I can use it to reward the people who help me and punish the ones who don't."

"You're both wrong," said the economist. "Money is the force that governs the world because it enables the free flow of goods and services from one person to another. That is the market, and the market rules human behavior."

The preacher frowned when he heard this. "Money is greed," he thundered from the pulpit. "The love of money is the root of all evil. It is easier for a camel to go through the eye of a needle than for a rich man to enter the kingdom of God." He said many other such things to his congregation, who weren't paying him what the preacher really wanted: attention.

The social scientist came up with her own theory. "Money," she wrote in her research paper, "is obligation. It's a series of promises made by one person to another, a social contract, the anonymity of which makes large-scale societies possible."

Groucho Marx could make neither head nor tail of this. "Money," he said, "frees you from doing the things you dislike. Since I dislike doing nearly everything, money is handy."

John and I recently attended a party hosted by a wealthy man who had built his dream mansion in the hills near Woodinville. We spent some time wandering the lovely grounds, which included a pond, a waterfall, and numerous themed gardens, all meticulously kept. Inside the mansion, we visited the guy's observatory, complete with Palomaresque telescope. Back out in the parking area, we examined an impressive building roofed with rows of solar panels. The building was bigger than our house. What it housed was a Porsche Panamera, the hybrid roadster with a base price of $96,000. We realized we were looking at the garage.

When we got home from the modern-day version of a royal soirée, we walked through our weed-strewn yard that neither of us had mowed since last May, climbed the wooden steps that needed painting but may have to do without for another year, and entered our humble home. "Here we are in our un-mansion with our un-millions," said John.

There are times when John expresses the wish that he could earn gobs of money so I can have everything my little heart desires. As a matter of fact, all the men in my family have, at one time or another, expressed the wish to give me a million dollars. It's always a million, too. Where they get that figure, I have no idea. Why one million? Why not two? Or even three?

In any case, it would be useless to give me a million dollars. I would simply go right out and buy a swamp. And why should I bother to own my own swamp when I already have one I can go to every day for free? Yesler Swamp and its drier counterpart, Montlake Fill, belong to all of us. We can go there any time we want and survey our domain.

That's exactly what I did one August morning last year. As I walked the Loop Trail just after dawn, the air already shimmered with heat waves, a harbinger of the scorcher predicted by the weather forecasters. On such days, I try to get out early, complete my circuit of the trail, and return home before the ambient temperature reaches my melting point, 82 degrees F. August heat, though, is well worth braving for the chance of seeing the shorebird migrants who stream south in vast numbers and sometimes stop for a rest and a bite on Main Pond.

Nothing stirred the still waters of the pond, but I was not overly disappointed. Tomorrow was another day, and shorebirds would be migrating for weeks to come.

Meanwhile, up in the tundra of the Far North, the wind was blowing steadily and sometimes fiercely. It ruffled the feathers of one Long-billed Dowitcher as he faced south, into the teeth of the wind. His mate stood nearby, her feet in one of the innumerable puddles that nourish the insect larvae hatching all across Alaska. It was the larvae that brought the dowitchers so far from their southern homes, to a feast for them and their chicks.

But food was not what the dowitchers had in mind now. They had done what they came here to do. Their babies, only a few days old, were already able to care for themselves. It was time for the parents to go.

Without a backward look, the male spread his wings, caught the wind, and flew. His mate watched him leave with no regrets, no memory even that will draw them back together again in the future. There will be plenty of dowitchers in the tundra for her to choose

Treasure

Long-billed Dowitcher ©Gregg Thompson

from next year. For now, she too felt the pull of migration, but she decided to catch another wind, another night.

A couple days later, the male arrived at the Fill in the full heat of summer. Another scorcher. The hot breeze ruffled his feathers as he stood with his long legs in the shallow waters of Main Pond. I found him there on the western shore, bobbing his head rapidly in and out of the water as he used his long, sensitive bill to hunt for larvae and crustaceans buried unseen in the mud.

He looked up at me when I slowly and carefully opened my camp stool and sat down to watch. The Northern Shovelers floating nearby scarcely bothered to turn their heads. They know people are no threat to them here, and somehow their peacefulness reassured the dowitcher. He studied me for a minute, then went back to stitching the mud. He had miles to go on his way south, but for now, there were critters to eat and safety among the ducks. If you're a dowitcher on migration in August—or a delighted birder on watch—that's all you need. Life is good.

Human beings can no longer live bare in nature as dowitchers do. We have come to rely too much on civilization.

We need clothes and shelter, food, water, transport, communication. In a post-industrial age, we can no longer make these things for ourselves. Instead, we consume them, giving in return the things that we ourselves can make. In my case, I make stories and books. My husband makes scientific theories and enterprises. The world places a certain value on these commodities and gives us money in exchange. We hope.

Like any other creature on Earth, we have the right to fight for our survival, which means, we have the right to consume resources. The question is: How many resources?

To answer that question, we must ask another: What constitutes survival? In nature, the answer is simple. Animals reproduce as many young as they can, in order to perpetuate the survival of their species. The young must find enough food and shelter to survive. In plentiful years, many young succeed. In lean years, many die. Nature strikes a harsh balance.

For humans, the equation is more complicated. Because we create so much of our own environment, we can protect ourselves from quite a bit of nature's harshness. How much protection we require depends on our definition of the good life.

Some of us define the good life by the amount of money we have, the kind of clothes we wear, the size of the house we live in. Status is important to human beings, and many of us think the best way to get some is to buy it. Or we seek power, another item for sale. Security, comfort, gratification, fun, luxury: all can be had with enough money. The list of such things is long.

As the world's population of humans swells to 12 billion or more, the way we each define the good life will have real and large impacts on ecology. It already does. Our challenge is to have a good life that is sustainable. Technology undoubtedly will provide many solutions to the problems we face in providing clean water, pure air, energy, and food to such a large number of people. But perhaps an equally important answer might lie in changing our focus from outward definitions of the good life to inward ones.

For all its power to impress, money is not the same thing as wealth, if we define wealth as an abundance of the things that make life worthwhile. It's true that I would like to have enough money to ensure that I do not become a burden on my children in later life. I would like to have enough comfort each day to put my feet up somewhere warm and dry, eat nourishing food that I cook myself, and wear shoes that don't leak. But for me, wealth consists of the love of my family, the strength of my friendships, the quality of my discourse, and the wonder I find in nature every single day.

I have thus defined my idea of the good life in a way that no amount of money can give me. Neither does money provide me with anything else I truly value. Status is something I bestow on myself when I ask if I have lived up to my ideals. The power I am most interested in is the power to direct my life in such a way that I gain wisdom from my successes and failures. For gratification and fun, I study nature and try to show other people how beautiful is this planet we share.

By this definition, the most valuable treasure of life is available to every one of us, greater than any wealth even the richest person could hoard. We already have the power to acquire it: It lies within.

Northern Shoveler © Tim Kuhn

26. Let It Go

If there's one thing birds know how to do, they know how to let go. One bird who is especially skilled at this is the mother Cooper's Hawk who appears at the Fill every fall with her annual supply of juveniles. She introduces them to their new dining room and then, when they aren't looking, she flies away, leaving her brood behind without a single regret.

She does not abandon them willy-nilly. On the contrary, she and her mate spend each spring and summer taking good care of the babies, brooding the eggs until they hatch, catching as much food as possible so the babies can grow heftier than their parents, waiting patiently while the kids learn how to fly. In short, each year the parents give their offspring the best possible start in life.

One year, the mother hawk dropped off three juveniles. The young hawks sat on perches around Main Pond, waiting for their mom to return and feed them, but she never did. At last, the hungry younglings began to hunt on their own, but they were pretty inept. The first one ended up in a tree with more than a hundred American Goldfinches perched above, just out of reach. The goldfinches weren't scared at all. They knew a hawk catches food with its feet, and how was this one going to do that, perched on a low branch? The second hawk scared up a Green Heron on Main Pond, but the heron was bigger than the hawk, so bejabbers. The third hawk started coursing after a Barn Swallow. I'm not absolutely sure the swallow even knew it was being chased. Swallows can fly at least twice as fast as Cooper's Hawks, and this swallow never even glanced back.

Finally, the three hawks gathered together on the willow snag to think about things. That's when they made their biggest mistake. A Belted Kingfisher flapped over from the canoe house, headed for her favorite fishing hole, Southwest Pond. All of a sudden, the three hawks rocketed forth from their tree, intent on capturing the kingfisher. The kingfisher gave one startled squawk and then did what all kingfishers would do in this situation. She lost her temper. Rattling off a series of unprintable phrases, she looped-a-loop behind the startled hawks and began pecking at them with her saber-like beak. The hawks tumbled through the air trying to escape. Eventually, the kingfisher flapped off, leaving the young hawks to preen their addled feathers back into order.

Lesson for the day: Never agitate a bird with a bigger beak and a meaner attitude than yours.

My first impulse, on watching this scenario, was to rush over to Safeway, buy a raw chicken, and throw it out near the hawks so they would have something to eat. I was afraid that otherwise, the kids would have to join the Breatharians, a cult whose members believe you can live by ingesting fresh air alone. But then I dimly recalled reading somewhere that many raptors are finicky about their food and won't eat anything unless they catch it themselves. I also wasn't sure the hawks would be able to recognize a Safeway chicken as food, plucked, plumped, and packaged as it would be.

That was three years ago, and I still think about those hawks. You see, unlike the mother Cooper's, I am not very skilled at letting go. On the contrary, I am what you might call a helicopter mom, hovering over my grown-up kids like a Sikorsky CH-53 Sea Stallion, instantly ready to drop supplies on their heads, or give them any other thing they might need. Whether they really need it or not.

I don't let go of my worries about other people who might need my help, either. Husband walking home in the rain? Ack, better go pick him up before he catches pneumonia. Best friend down with the flu? Ack, better make a dinner and run it over to her house right away so her family won't go hungry. Better yet, make two dinners. Maybe three. Neighbor's garbage not out by the curb at 7 a.m. on pickup day? Ack, better haul it out for him before the garbage truck skips his house.

My worry centers have always been on the far end of the human continuum, out there where normal starts to shade into hmm. Somewhere along the line, though, they got turned on permanently, and I wanted to figure out how to shut them off.

I decided counseling was in order, so I called my therapist-in-waiting, Dr. Phil, and made an appointment. Phil and I go back a ways. I like him because he is willing to address my problems with practical advice, and he never talks about Freudian cigars. My husband says seeing Phil is like going to a spa for the brain. I think of it more as a realignment of my mental tires.

"So, Phil," I said, after telling him about my current fix-up need, "what do you suggest?"

Phil thought for a moment, and then he gently said, "Sometimes the best way to turn off a worry is to give your mind a break. You can do this by finding an activity or a place where you aren't thinking about your worries every second. Do you have an activity or place where this already happens for you?"

"Sure I do. I go to Montlake Fill and look at birds. When I'm there, I never think about my troubles."

"Good, good," murmured Phil. Therapists always murmur. "How often do you go, and how long do you spend?"

"I go every day," I said, "and I usually spend three hours. Sometimes more."

Phils eyes bugged out. "Whoa, I was thinking more about ten or fifteen minutes a couple times a week," he gasped. His tone said the rest: If worries were elephants in the room, I'd be hosting a circus.

Actually, since that day, I don't. Now, whenever my worry centers start churning out scenarios, I picture Phil's bulging eyes, and I start to laugh. Laughing is a surefire cure for worries. But it's not just that. Phil made me realize how it is that I find peace of mind at the Fill.

Birding at the Fill keeps me engaged in the moment. When I connect with nature, I occupy a context bigger than myself. There

Belted Kingfisher © Thomas Sanders

are a million things to see and think about, but not a single one I *must* see or think about. There are no deadlines to keep. No past to drag me backwards. No future to push me down with worst-case imaginings. I lose the part of myself that cares for such things, and thus I free my soul to be joyful.

One day last winter, I was walking the Loop Trail in the middle of a howling windstorm. A cottonwood, weakened by age and inner rot, had crashed across the trail before I arrived. Its dead branches reached out like emaciated fingers trying to snatch all life from anyone foolish enough to be caught in its death throes.

Seeing the carnage left behind, the fallen giant with its broken limbs, I laughed into the wind, not for the futility of the tree but for the life still vivid all around me and in me, for the wild that will always remain. I was alone except for the wind, until I heard the high-pitched calls of the Golden-crowned Kinglets who forage here in flocks when the weather turns cold. Their songs engulfed me, pure sound carried in waves through the air, like piccolos dancing. I turned round and round, trying to see them. At last, the flock appeared amid the branches of the downed tree. The males' orange and gold crowns were raised, whether by wind or my presence, I do not know. But in the gray light of the storm, they glowed like living embers, sparks of life darting here and there, never stopping.

For a moment, oh one moment, I joined the flock, knew the feel of the bare branch, the strength of my own muscles, the freedom to let the wild whirl me away like a kinglet in the storm. All I had to do was let go. I opened my arms and flew.

27. Faith in Your Feathers

The two Killdeers who have laid claim to the gravel road next to the Youth Farm were on patrol the other day, marching back and forth in the short grass sprouting amid the pebbles. I'm sure they're the same two who raised a couple of chicks here last spring, but now that it's September, why they are still acting like they have a nest to protect is a mystery.

Their behavior may be due to recrudescence, a phenomenon that sometimes affects birds in the fall. The length of days and nights mimics spring, leading some birds to think they should start getting romantic ideas. For Killdeers, thoughts of love are closely tied to claims of territory, and these two have staked out a wide swath. When I inadvertently crossed the boundary, they swarmed around me like MPs at a checkpoint, yelling at me to go away or else.

Ordinarily, when I find I am bothering birds in their natural habitat, I leave. I figure I'm in their home, and they should be allowed to make the rules. Besides, after years of political doorbelling and yard-signing, not to mention Girl Scout cookie-selling, I know when I'm not welcome. Usually in those circumstances, I move on to the next venue without demur. But Killdeers have expansive ideas about their home territories. I've had Killdeers chase me halfway around the Loop Trail, alerting all and sundry to hide from this dangerous, bipedal interloper with the floppy hat and the high-powered optics. Their voices are piercing and loud, their manners pushy and rude. When they get revved up, all the other birds within hearing distance disappear. It's annoying.

I remonstrated. "Look," I said, trying to reason with them, "I didn't know you were here. I just want to scan for pipits and sparrows. I won't bother you. Now be quiet."

But as all birders know, reasoning with Killdeers is about as effective as using logic on a Labrador retriever, a dog who cheerfully will *try* to make out what you're saying but, with an IQ in the single digits, simply cannot. Your words enter one ear, skitter around for a while without denting a single neuron, then exit out the other ear, leaving behind no impression whatever.

"Ki-ki-ki-killeer," the Killdeers clucked, pattering around my feet like ankle-biters trying to choose the right spot to bite.

I was about to advance another argument, when suddenly the Barn Swallows soaring overhead gave their distinctive, two-note alarm call. The Killdeers and I froze, knowing a raptor was near. Sure enough, a Merlin rocketed past at head height, its wings bent back like a fighter jet on afterburners. After it passed, I glanced down at the Killdeers at my feet. They weren't moving a muscle. These normally twitchy, can't-sit-still birds might as well have been stuffed, they were so immobile. The Merlin cruised back, its ominous shadow skimming the short grass like Death's scythe.

A juicy Killdeer would have made a perfect meal for the falcon, and my two compadres knew it. So they stayed absolutely still, counting on their brown, white, and black feathers to blend into the background, making them invisible. In reality, they were out in the open in plain view. If they had moved, they would have died. But they had faith in their feathers, and the Shadow of Death passed over them harmlessly.

In this age of the Great Recession, when forces beyond our control deprive us of our homes, denude us of our hard-won savings, demote us to jobs that fail to pay a living wage—if we can find jobs at all—it can seem that we are powerless to shape our own future.

My 97-year-old Aunt Marie lived through just such a time herself. She graduated from teachers' college in South Bend, Indiana, at the height of the Great Depression. In all her class, only one graduate found a job, and that was the daughter of the mayor. Marie went

Merlin © Doug Parrott

out job-hunting every day for four years. To save the nickel it cost her to ride the streetcar, she walked miles everywhere. Occasionally, she would find temporary work, enough to give her parents a few dollars to defray the cost of her keep. But invariably, times would worsen, and Marie would be out on the streets again.

Then in 1941, the Japanese bombed Pearl Harbor, Franklin Roosevelt declared war, and men by the thousands signed up to fight for their country. Marie's best friend called her from Seattle. "Boeing is hiring women," she reported. "Come out here right away."

Marie's friend knew that Marie had never wanted to be a teacher. She had always yearned for a career in engineering, but women weren't accepted in that man's world. "I always loved engines and tools," Marie told me. "But my mother never let me take shop classes in school. She said it was unladylike. So when I learned that one of the biggest aerospace companies in the country was hiring women, I got on the next train."

When she arrived in Seattle, she went to the Boeing employment center and took the standard aptitude test given to all potential

Killdeer © Kathrine Lloyd

employees. She got the highest mechanical aptitude score Boeing had ever seen. They hired her on the spot, put her through a crash course in technical writing at the University of Washington, and got her started writing technical manuals on how to put together the airplanes needed for the war effort. Marie began a technical writing career that lasted for the next 40 years. "I always knew I could do something good in engineering," she said.

Marie had faith in her feathers.

Mind you, she was scarred by those bad times. She came out of them believing that an individual has little control over the large events of the world. The best strategy, in her experience, was to roll with the punches, take the blows of fate with easy acceptance, not fight against forces larger than you. In her view, knowing what you are capable of does not necessarily mean the world will give you a chance to shine. It might slam the door in your face or open it wide—capricious, either way.

Marie used to criticize me for my political activism. She thought it was arrogant of me and my Baby Boom generation to believe we could change the world in ways that we decided were best. She and I used to argue about it.

"When Socrates was condemned to death for corrupting the young," I pontificated to her one day, having recently studied ancient Greek philosophy in school, "and his students offered to smuggle him to freedom, he refused. He believed you should stay and fight to change the country you love."

"Socrates was forced to drink hemlock and die," Aunt Marie mildly replied.

Toward the end of her life, she in her 90s, I in my 60s, we returned to our old argument. "You may have been right to fight against the status quo," she said, much to my surprise. "Maybe if my generation had fought harder, we could have created more opportunities for women, lessened racial prejudice, and given civil rights to more people. Your generation did that."

"But I admire your attitude about accepting the things we can't change," I said, thinking of the many battles I have lost over the years and the heartbreak they have cost me. "Now I understand why the salmon who swim upstream get so raggedy and die right after spawning. They're pooped."

Marie just smiled and said nothing. It was her way of encouraging me to think more and talk less. Since then, I have thought a lot about faith in your feathers, in other words, about confidence in your own strength and in a hopeful future. Faith, you see, does not rule out failure. No matter how much you believe, no matter how much you strive, you might fail. Does that invalidate your beliefs; should that weaken your strength?

I don't see that any given success or failure is relevant to the truth of your beliefs, as long as you have built your beliefs upon wisdom and with humility. The things you believe in, and the confidence you have in those beliefs, are the very definition of faith, and faith will give you the strength to keep swimming upstream despite all the boulders that may lie in your way.

Hub McCann, as played by Robert Duvall in the film *Secondhand Lions,* tried to convey this to his young nephew in a memorable scene. The nephew had been raised by a mom who told him nothing but lies. Now he wanted only the truth from the adults in his life. He had heard stories about the heroic exploits his uncle had performed in Africa, and he wanted Hub to swear they were true.

Hub refused. He told the boy it didn't matter if the stories were true or not. When his disbelieving nephew said the truth meant everything, Hub explained, "Sometimes the things that may or may not be true are the things a man needs to believe in the most. That people are basically good; that honor, courage, and virtue mean everything; that power and money, money and power mean nothing; that good always triumphs over evil; and I want you to remember this, that love—true love—never dies.... Doesn't matter if it's true or not. You see, a man should believe in those things, because those are the things worth believing in."

You are stronger than you know. Have faith in your feathers.

28. Dumb and Dumber

During the warm days of early October, the Turkey Vultures from British Columbia migrate south, passing over the Fill in flocks called kettles. The vultures like to wait until the Sun heats up the air and the temperature gets hot. Then they spring into the sky, stretch out wings that can span up to six feet, and flap laboriously into the sky.

Once airborne, they seek out thermal columns of warm air that rise from the heated land. If they can find such an air column, they fly into it, hold their wings steady, and spiral effortlessly upward, sometimes thousands of feet high. At the top of the thermal, the vultures exit their elevator and zoom down an invisible slope of air, traveling miles without a single wing-flap.

The other day, I saw six vultures circling overhead, rising higher with each circuit. Other Turkey Vultures hustled over from all parts north, eager to join their fellows and ride the thermal that had formed over Husky Stadium. Like a flash mob, the flock grew and grew. I felt myself standing on tiptoe, longing to join this living tornado, yearning to feel the wind lift my pied black-and-white wings, wishing I could master the skies as they did. In all, eighteen vultures spiraled around and around in their kettle, then disappeared out of sight, taking my longing with them.

Most people feel a bit uneasy around vultures. When they see one, they crack jokes about the need to stay upright and keep moving. Then they laugh self-consciously and twitch.

It is true that Turkey Vultures are unlovely raptors who don't quite fit the paradigm of fierce, wild, and free—the characteristics that so pervasively embody our image of other birds of prey in the raptor family such as eagles, falcons, and hawks. Vultures "prey" on carrion. They are featherless—quite bald except for a few odd bristles—from head to neck, supposedly to facilitate hygiene. I guess when you dine by sticking your head as far as it can go into a carcass that has seen better days, you don't want to mess up your hairdo. Better to have no do at all.

But I've had a soft spot in my heart for vultures ever since I attended a raptor show at Woodland Park Zoo. The zookeepers have

Turkey Vulture © Tim Kuhn

trained their raptors to perch on a wrist. When the keeper flings the bird up, it spreads out its magnificent wings and flies toward a piece of meat mounted on a stick at the other end of the birds' enclosure. It's very impressive.

On this particular day, the keepers decided to bring out Modoc the Vulture. Like all the other raptors, Modoc sat quietly on his keeper's gloved wrist until the keeper flung him up. Modoc didn't really want to go—vultures value their rest and relaxation. But what choice had he? Up he went, flapping his massive wings much harder than he liked, and off he disappeared into the distance. The crowd was silent. The keeper was silent. We all waited for Modoc to reappear, but he never did.

"Well," hemmed his keeper, "Modoc's a slow learner. We're still trying to teach him to fly to the post over there. But he doesn't always remember to do that." Then she added in a hopeful but unsure tone, "He'll return when he gets hungry."

I was utterly charmed. Modoc's combination of stupidity and independence appealed to me, I suppose because I also live dumb and free. The freedom to be dumb, after all, gives you permission to start over, to be the beginner, to learn something new without fear.

Young children, of course, know this instinctively. They are completely unafraid to learn new things, even preposterous new things, such as how to graduate from crawling safely on all fours to walking precariously while balanced on two little feet. They fall down a lot at first, but they just pick themselves up and try again. Next thing we parents know, they're walking all over the house, extending their quest for knowledge with experiments that cause us to clutch our heads and moan.

I remember when our oldest son reached this stage. It coincided with a period of some months when I could not keep a toothbrush in the house. I'd stagger into the bathroom each morning, grope for my toothbrush in the cup, and discover it had disappeared. Marching into the bedroom, I would rouse my sleeping husband and demand to know what he had done with my toothbrush. "Nothing," he would protest. "I never touched it."

I found this hard to believe. My husband is the typical absent-minded professor. When he starts thinking of physics, anything can happen. It took no stretch of my imagination to picture him standing at the sink, brushing his teeth with my toothbrush. Suddenly, a physics neuron fires. John starts thinking about a calculation, wanders off, toothbrush still clutched in hand, and presto! instant disappearance of said brush.

"Not so," John said, when I told him my theory. "I always put my toothbrush in the same cup as my shaving brush. The brushes are hence unitary, which simplifies my life."

But the next day, I'd find my toothbrush gone again. This went on for weeks until the morning when I staggered into the bathroom and saw my little son climbing down from the sink, my toothbrush clutched in his hand. He toddled over to the furnace duct, stuck the toothbrush through the grate, and pushed.

"Ack," I yelled, and my little scientist turned his inquisitive eyes to a new project, this one in the field of sociology. He learned that day about how to make your mother crazy. He also learned where toothbrushes go when you fill up an air duct with them. We managed to fish out a dozen or so, but I bet even now, years later, when the new owners turn on the furnace and the smell of toothpaste wafts through the house, they wonder where the room deodorizer is. I hope they like mint.

Adults seldom learn like this. We're too afraid to try something new just to see what happens. I guess we've seen too many results of the dire things that can happen in this life. Or maybe we're more afraid of failure, fearful that other people will think we're stupid. Or we're too caught up in the day-to-day ado of our busy lives to take time out to feel the slow, lazy pleasure of learning something by trial and error.

Rather than "go back to kindergarten and start at the bottom," we often push our ignorance off onto others. We pay people to fix things or grow things or cook things for us because we've forgotten how, or perhaps we never learned. After all, why take the time to figure out how a computer operating system really works when you can ask your youngest child to install the latest version of the software and have you up and running in just a few hours? That's what I do. And if the system crashes, I just call him up and ask him to repair whatever broke.

"You really should learn more about computers," he gently tells me from time to time. "They're a part of your everyday life, and you need to know how they work."

I agree with him out loud, but really what I'm thinking is: What a colossal waste of time it would be to cram all this technical gibble-gabble into my short-term memory cells when I know perfectly well that my aging neurons are going to forget it as soon as the test is over. Besides, learning that stuff would mean I would have to overcome my considerable fear of computers.

Still, my son has a point. I really should take more responsibility to master the tools of daily life. They keep getting more complicated every year, and if I don't keep up, eventually I will find myself living in a world that might as well be governed by black magic.

I remind myself of something my 97-year-old aunt used to say: "The more you learn about something, the more interesting it becomes." Right.

"I can do this," I say, starting up my computer and clicking on a new program. "I love learning. Computers are fun. Every child can learn." Other adages come to mind, such as this favorite from the surfers: "If you look at the rocks, that's what you'll hit; if you look at the waves, that's what you'll surf."

Not that I ever want to go surfing. Too cold, too wet, too much water up the nose. But I understand what the surfers are getting at. To learn anything new, you must keep your eyes on the prize you want to win, not focus on the failure you might achieve instead.

I recite one last adage, a mantra my husband chants whenever he tries to teach me anything technological: They want you to succeed. I call up my son. "Okay," I say, "please teach me how to upload high-quality photos onto my website." And so back to kindergarten.

Recently, I went to the Woodland Park Zoo website to find out if Modoc was still alive. Turkey Vultures in captivity can live for more than 30 years, so I thought perhaps Modoc was still entertaining his many fans. It turns out he is. The zoo has posted a YouTube video showing Modoc's latest skill. Modoc's keeper stands in the doorway of the raptor house and urges Modoc to come out. Nothing happens at first, but eventually, Modoc waddles out the door and heads over to the keeper, who gives him a pellet of vulture chow as she tells the crowd about vultures.

"Vultures are nature's recyclers," she says, as Modoc strolls behind her, hoping for more chow. Soon they come to a paper cup on the grass, next to a blue recycling bin. "Now, Modoc is going to show us how we might recycle something," says the keeper.

Modoc picks up the cup and carries it to the recycling bin. Clearly, he's supposed to put the cup in the bin, but instead, he drops it. Then he looks at the bin, as if wondering what the heck it's doing there. He pecks at the cup, looks at the bin, steps on the cup, walks over to the bin and looks in, then investigates the cup to see if any vulture chow has appeared yet. No food having shown up, Modoc starts to lose interest. But the keeper stays on him. "Come on, Moe," she says in an encouraging voice, "you know what to do."

But Modoc doesn't.

"He's taking his time today," chirps the keeper to the crowd, as Modoc plays with the cup some more. "Vultures are very curious birds," she says. "They don't really know what's food and what's not food. They don't want to eat something that's still alive."

I could tell the keeper is beginning to run out of patter. She looks a little nervous. Finally, Modoc picks up the cup with his beak, hops onto the edge of the bin, and drops it in. "Good job, good job!" praises the keeper in a high-pitched, kindergartner tone, giving Moe a treat.

Her voice sounds eerie to me. It's the same tone my youngest son uses when I manage to upload one photo onto my website. "Good job!" he says. I find myself looking around for a pellet to swallow.

29. Airs and Graces

To see a Western Grebe floating serenely on the lake, its long white neck punctuated by the black comma of its head and nape, is to see grace itself come to life.

"Grace" is an odd word in our language. It comes from the Latin word *gratis,* meaning "a pleasing quality." Over the centuries, as Latin became more vulgar and eventually turned into French, the "pleasing quality" of grace came to mean "elegance of form" or "beauty of movement." Along its way toward elegance and beauty, though, grace took a turn toward good will and also came to mean "favor" or "gratitude." That is why devout people say grace before a meal and also why they pray for grace from God.

For me, the Western Grebes who grace the waters of Union Bay embody all the definitions of the word. They fill my eyes with elegance and my soul with gratitude, whether they are fishing for minnows or floating with their bills tucked into their backs for a nap.

Two Western Grebes have settled into the cove nearest Conibear Shellhouse this past fall. There they dive for fish in the morning and go to sleep in the afternoon. My husband John was the first in our family to see them. He had been walking home from campus after work one afternoon and crossed the dock in front of the shellhouse, where the UW's championship rowers train for regattas. He says he likes to walk out onto the dock to survey the lake here, but really what he likes best is to recall the time he was scared nearly witless by three coyotes. John had been thinking about physics and was paying no attention to anything around him until he set foot on the dock and glanced up. Facing him were three snarling coyotes. Each one was circling around and around, tail waving in the breeze. They looked worse than mean. They looked rabid.

Slowly, John reached into his shirt pocket for his cell phone to call security. Then he noticed something wasn't quite right about the coyotes. Although they were moving briskly, they had no legs. None at all. It turns out the Facilities Department had mounted coyote models onto steel poles so they could twirl in the breeze and scare away Canada Geese. The geese, of course, had figured out more quickly than John that they had nothing to fear from these canine whirligigs and had proceeded about their business, making deposits for the rowers to step in.

Whenever John needs a laugh, he stops by the dock to see if the coyote merry-go-round is on duty. One afternoon when he passed by, the coyotes were missing but two Western Grebes were asleep on the dark water, floating like two white scoops of ice cream in a glass of root beer. Quickly, John hauled out his phone and called me up. "Come over here right away!" he breathed softly into the phone so as not to disturb the birds. "I'll be waiting for you on the dock."

I leaped into the car and headed out. Western Grebes are becoming scarcer by the decade. No one knows exactly why. They used to be common at the Fill, but now years go by without me seeing a single one. To have two at once is just unheard-of.

When I got to the parking lot, I grabbed my binoculars and dashed down the hill to the dock, trying to look unthreatening in case the grebes had awakened. As I ran past John, who was seated in front of the open doors of the shellhouse, I glanced into the building and skidded to a halt. Thirty half-naked male rowers were stroking their oars in unison on rowing machines lined up from one end of the building to the other. Each male had the physique of Ben Hur.

I glanced over to the water, and there were the grebes. I looked at the crew, whose sweaty muscles were rippling. Guys, grebes, grebes, guys. I didn't know who to look at first, or most. My head was ticktocking back and forth like a metronome. It was the only time in my life I can remember wishing I were a chameleon, because chameleons have eyes that can each move independently. Unlike humans, chameleons have no trouble looking at two things at once.

During one of my ocular oscillations, my eyes happened to light on my husband, who was clutching his sides and laughing. I started to turn red, but he graciously said, "It's all nature, you know."

"Gracious" is another word that derives from grace. In our modern vernacular, it has come to mean charming politeness, the kind you might find in royal circles perhaps, or in the Deep South. Graciousness is far more than simply good manners, however, as John demonstrated at the shellhouse. It's also a willingness to accept people's imperfections.

"A gracious person can turn the other cheek when someone is rude, and smile and return kindness," says my friend Lili Mounce. Lili is founder of "creative savv," a blog about how to live well and frugally.* She believes that graciousness is an issue deeply related to quality of life, but she isn't talking about money. On the contrary, Lili is devoted to the idea that we can live far better on far less than we might imagine.

"A person who is living graciously on less is simply one with deep gratitude for the myriad blessings in life, in spite of his or her economic status," she says. "A gracious person accepts a wilted handful of yard weeds from a small child with heartfelt thanks. We've all seen a gracious loser before. He's the one who offers his hand with a smile and congratulates the one who bested him. A truly gracious person finds the good in all people, regardless of their income, appearance, or the work they do."

Finding the good in other people isn't always easy. Sometimes you have to dig for it like the farmboy who assiduously shoveled through a giant pile of manure in the barn stall. When asked why he had taken on such an odoriferous job, he replied, "With all this horse manure, I figure there's got to be a pony in here somewhere."

When we dig deep enough to find the common humanity in our foes—for that pony is indeed in there somewhere—and when we

---

*url: http://creativesavv.blogspot.com

Western Grebe ©Doug Parrott

find it within our hearts to respect that humanity, then we become completely unable to demonize the other. Instead, we are forced to acknowledge, "You are like me." Since you are like me, then you must have the same inherent needs as I do: the need to find enough to eat, live in decent shelter, create a family to love, stick loyally to your beliefs, and be willing to fight for the things you care about.

But true graciousness teaches us that this level of understanding is only the first step. A deeper and more important step is to be able to recognize, "I am like you." When you can say this to other people, you are conveying your wish to enter their world and walk in their shoes for a while, so that you may understand why their ideas differ from yours and why those ideas might have value. You may still end up dealing with wide chasms of difference, but you will also be building bridges.

The other day, I was out at the Fill birding with a friend. We watched an immature eagle come blasting across the lake, scattering coots in all directions. Wheeling in a tight circle, the eagle swooped back and forth over the panicked coots, diving close to the water to make a pass, then flapping high into the sky to stoop again in freefall, her enormous talons extended. Long minutes went by as the drama played out. Finally, the eagle made one last plunge, all the way into the water, and a hapless coot, too worn out to escape, succumbed. The eagle floated on the lake for a few minutes, catching her breath, than laboriously she slapped her massive wings against the water and rose into the air, the dead coot dangling from her claws.

As she flew to the nearest mud island, two adult Bald Eagles came screaming toward her, intent on robbing the immature of her hard-won prize. Quickly, the immature snatched up her coot and fled, but the adults caught up to her and started dive-bombing. In short order, the immature dropped her prey, which an adult grabbed in midair. Then all the eagles flew away.

"Hm," I ruminated to my friend, "those adults were probably her own parents."

"I suppose now you'll write something mushy about cold-hearted parent birds mistreating their kids, just like some human parents do," said my friend. She is a scientist and prefers to keep her distance from emotions when in the field or the lab.

"Well, it's true I am a romantic, not a scientist like you," I admitted defensively, trying not to let my little feelings be hurt. "Still, my observations of birds in the field are meticulous."

We walked along silently for a time. I remembered John's example of graciousness. Perhaps I needed to consider my friend's criticism more seriously—dig around until I found the truth in the point she had made. Maybe I *should* unpurple my prose. Make it more scientific, less sentimental. Scale it back to lavender, maybe. At the very least, perhaps I could find a way to bridge the gap between science and art.

"You're right that we shouldn't anthropomorphize birds," I finally said, "and I try not to. In fact, I don't honestly think birds are like us. On the other hand, we are like birds. We both have to survive hard times, eat enough food, drink enough water, attract a mate, raise a family. By understanding the needs we share with wild animals, perhaps we will become more aware of our responsibility to them and to the planet. Maybe we will stop thinking of ourselves as the apex of creation, entitled to grab all the bounty of nature for ourselves because we can. Animals that took millions of years to evolve to this point, on this day, in this place—or, if you're religious, were created by God himself—deserve their place in the Sun, too."

On that note, we parted, she to return to her science lab, I to climb down from my soapbox and return to wild nature, a world I hope will never be controlled or even fully understood by us. A world where grace is bestowed without stint, to my everlasting and heartfelt gratitude.

And where I wonder how old John and I will have to be until we can move in with the kids and start stealing their food.

Least Sandpiper © Kathrine Lloyd

30. The Age of Dinosaurs

The birds of the Fill are not avi-kingdom's earliest risers. In fact, contrary to how all the field guides say birds should behave, ours do not spring up off their perches to greet the predawn with a chorus of songs and perky cheeps. With the exception of a few over-eager robins and the occasional gung-ho wren, Fill birds can't seem to muster even a grumpy squawk in the dawn's early light. They prefer to sleep in.

I can sympathize. While I do usually get up before dawn, I am not an early-morning get-out-of-the-houser. On chill autumn mornings, the heater is too cozy, the coffee too hot. The *Times* crossword calls to me, and all too frequently I answer. It's hard to face the cold, dank chill of the fog that often blankets Seattle in the fall. Much easier to spread an afghan over my feet, pull out the footrest of my Barcalounger, and lean back in total comfort. Ah, civilization.

But then I start to hear a little voice in my head. It belongs to Ricky Young, famous Washington surfer. He is saying, "If you do nothing, nothing happens. If you do something, something happens." His voice echoes Debi Shearwater's. Debi is one of the world's foremost seabird experts. She leads pelagic expeditions out of Monterey. She begins to chant into my mental ear, "If you snooze, you lose."

Right. Birds have flown to the Fill in the night. There is no telling what might await me. Time to force myself to hit the trail. I lower the lounger and put away the paper. I need to see.

If my friends' voices manage to blast me out of the house before dawn, I am treated to sights so celestial they make the world look as if heaven itself had descended to visit the Earth for a short time. The Sun, too delicate to glare from on high, shines a soft glow of pale gold over the land. The waters of Water Lily Cove smoke with mist. Each blade of grass is beaded with diamond drops, each stone on the path casts a soft shadow.

As I walk toward the shore, the world gradually wakes up. A Red-tailed Hawk shakes out his feathers, spreads his wings, and glides over the field. A Least Sandpiper who has migrated during the night manages to catch a large bug in the mud of Main Pond, a welcome meal on its brief stopover before it takes flight again for California. The sparrows who have been gathering the grass seeds in the field around the Lone Pine Tree for the past few weeks begin to arrive. They eye me warily when I set down my camp stool, but after a little while, they allow me to join the flock. It is so still, I can hear their little feet scrape against the grass as they search for seeds. It is a crackly, homey kind of sound, very comforting to the ear.

It is pleasant to sit on my stool and watch others work. I never used to be able to do this. If anyone around me was hard at work on anything, I would feel compelled to jump up and help. But in recent years, my ability to jump—upwards or in any other direction—has declined, making it possible for me to rest my bones without guilt. In fact, I have reached the age when it is tempting to ease up on the many demands the world makes of me. After all, I have worked hard most of my life. I deserve respite from my cares, don't I? Perhaps what I really deserve is a retirement home. The ones that advertise on the internet trumpet the fact that living in their complexes is care-free. No lawns to mow. No weeds to pull. No screaming children to disturb the placid flow of life in the golden years. "You deserve the best," says one ad.

But is it? Defining the best at this age is just as difficult as it was to define when I was young. Back then, I struggled to figure out what career I was qualified for and whether I would like it. I wondered if I would ever find the love of my life and get married, or if I should just throw in the towel and start acquiring multiple cats. I wasn't sure if I ever wanted kids. I couldn't decide if my dream home was shaped like the Space Needle or Mrs. Piggle-Wiggle's upside-down house. Thank God most of those questions were answered long ago, though I still sometimes wonder about the house.

Lately I have spent a good deal of time talking to friends who are slightly older than I am. "How do you like retirement?" I ask them. "What do you spend your time doing?"

I get a variety of answers. Some of my friends are just glad to put their feet up and rest from the hurly-burly of a world that beat them up a lot more than they ever wanted. Others are taking the chance to do things they always wished to do but never had the time or money before: travel, learn piano, study German. Most of them say they've never been busier or happier in all their lives. "What are you going to do?" they ask me.

I shake my head. Despite my diminishing abilities to leap like a young salmon anymore, I still can't quite wrap my mind around retiring. I don't really want to quit working. I don't want to let go of deadlines to meet, challenges to face. I don't even want to give up the fight to conquer the weeds in my yard, though I have to admit they have defeated me every one of the past 29 years I have fought them. If I move to a retirement complex where gardeners come twice a week to make the yard all pretty, my weeds will have won.

No, I want to stay engaged in the messy, noisy fray of life. Heaven does not yet equal haven for me. Still, it's probably a good idea to do some planning ahead. So recently, I met with two financial advisors to talk about my retirement plans. "I've been conducting an experiment for the past year," I told them. "I've tried to live on the income I think we will get when we stop getting a regular paycheck. I want to see if we can do it comfortably."

"That's awesome," one of them said. Awesome? I realized a dreaded moment in life had arrived: the time when your caregivers and advisors are so much younger than you, they look like high school freshmen. As you gaze into their cherubic faces, you know they never heard of Bob Dylan, the Three Stooges, Ed Sullivan, or any of the other icons of your youth. How can hatchlings as young as these ever hope to understand me?

Still, I had made the appointment. I forged ahead. "Yes, awesome is the word, thanks. I made a yearly budget," I said and gave them a figure that was roughly 20 percent above the poverty line for two adults living in Seattle. That seemed reasonable to me, an amount that would keep us solidly in the middle class.

The two girls looked at each other. "That's a pretty small budget. Are you sure you included everything?"

I assured them I had.

"What about your gym membership?" one asked. "People often forget to include that." They chuckled condescendingly, I suppose because people their age forget only the things they want to, not the essentials, such as where you put your bifocals.

"We don't belong to a gym," I answered.

"How about your monthly cable bill?" the other asked.

"We don't have cable."

"Did you include vacations and get-aways?"

"We don't take vacations, and we never get away."

"Eating out?"

"We seldom do that, either." I had been gazing up at the ceiling as they asked me these questions, trying to figure out what our expenses really were in the areas they were asking about. When I finally lowered my eyes, I saw they were looking at me in horror.

Their faces reminded me of the look on my mother-in-law's face when she told me about a farmwife who had gone berserk in Iowa one day and had shot up the barn. My mother-in-law was a family-practice attorney in a small town. She was hired by the farmwife's husband to represent his wife at the involuntary commitment examination she was due to undergo. "Well, Chet," my mother-in-law said, "what do you think made your wife take your shotgun out and blast holes in the barn?"

Chet scratched his grizzled head. "I dunno," he said, completely baffled. "She ain't been off the farm in 30 years, and she never done that before."

"Look," I hastened to explain to my would-be financiers before they could mention anything about the possibility of my own invol-

The Age of Dinosaurs

Red-winged Blackbird © Doug Parrott

untary commitment, due to the deep rut I lived in, "my husband and I lead a very rich life. We are both engaged in starting new businesses. I've just started my own publishing house and am writing my third nature book. My husband is working on inventions that will change the way the world approaches healing. We don't have cable because we aren't interested in wasting time watching TV. We don't take vacations because what vacation could ever be more fun than working on our dreams? We don't go to the gym because we walk every day in one of the most spectacular birding spots on the West Coast, the Montlake Fill. We don't really want to retire because we're having too much fun!"

"This is beyond our experience," one of the girls said. "We'll have to send your file to our supervisor. He'll call you soon."

But he never did. I guess we were beyond his experience, too.

Back at the Fill, I ambled along the Loop Trail, stopping frequently to set up my camp stool and rest my aching knees. The Sun broke through the mist and warmed my shoulders, making me feel glad to be alive. As the air got hot, so too did the male Red-winged Blackbirds perched on top of the cattails, swelling themselves up to the size of Chihuahuas in preparation for a loud blast of bagpipe music designed to flatten any rivals brazen enough to respond.

Usually when I am out in nature, I try my best to blend in, to connect with the wild, and abandon the works of humanity. But on this day, I felt grateful for civilization. Birds in the wild never grow old. As soon as they start to sicken or weaken, the predators who are always on the lookout for laggards move in. We humans carry the burden of old age, both when we are young and must care for the old, and when we are old and must let others care for us. The burden can feel heavy at times, but it has its glories too.

My beloved 97-year-old aunt used to say, "Every decade is happier than the one before." She taught me that the golden years are to be treasured just as much as every other stage of life; more, perhaps, as the long days grow short.

31. The Comedy Cat Won't Go in the Tragedy Bag

Like fog caressing moss, like smoke wafting over trees, the Barred Owl floated noiselessly to her favorite perch in the swamp: a cottonwood nook hidden from the prying eyes of her enemies, the crows. Wrapping her needle-sharp talons around a branch, the owl folded her enormous wings along her back and blinked sleepy eyes. Dawn was just breaking. The Sun's corona nibbled at the houses lining the top of the ridge to the east. It had been a good night of hunting: one unwary rat and a tasty vole, enough to keep the owl satisfied until the Moon rose again. She puffed out all her feathers and shook them a little, like a woman putting her curls into order. She would do a full preen when she awoke again at dusk. For now, she was tired. It was time to rest. Her eyes slowly closed.

For the first time in history, Barred Owls have come to Yesler Swamp, the easternmost part of Montlake Fill. I saw my first one on October 23, 2011. I was sitting at an outdoor table in the parking lot of the Center for Urban Horticulture, checking people in as they gathered for a guided walk sponsored by Friends of Yesler Swamp. The walk was led by UW biology professor Joe Ammirati, famous for his wide knowledge of native mushrooms. We had a good crowd, which was not surprising, considering how many people nowadays are interested in harvesting wild mushrooms.

Barred Owl © Doug Parrott

Everything was proceeding apace, when my birder friend Woody Wheeler emerged from the swamp and called out, "Did you see that Barred Owl on the trail? Isn't it great?"

"Barred Owl? Where?" I screeched. I leaped to my feet. Pencils and registration forms flew in all directions.

"Near the big cottonwood tree, where the trail turns south toward Yesler Cove," said Woody. "The owl is perched on a branch next to a tree trunk."

"Register yourselves!" I shouted to the startled mushroom people still waiting in line and shot off down the trail. I think a few stray forms swirled in the vortex I left behind. I wasn't about to miss the first Barred Owl ever seen at the Fill.

Rounding the trail, I started scanning the cottonwoods for a pile of lumpy gray feathers amid the equally lumpy gray piles of dead leaves and sticks collecting in the tree's branches. One pile moved. It opened two black eyes, eyes with no visible pupil or any white rim, eyes like two lumps of living coal, like burning tar that gives heat but no light, like the dark gates of the Netherworld opening into infinity.

The owl and I locked eyes. In hers I could see nothing—or everything. In hers I was lost.

I remain lost to this day—lost in wonder that such a magical creature exists at all; lost in gratitude that Woody was generous about sharing his sighting, and so was the owl; lost in sheer joy every time I recall the feeling of connection I made with something so wild and mysterious.

But also lost in ambiguity, for Barred Owls are invaders from the East who threaten the survival of our native forest raptors, the Spotted Owls. Barred Owls have been expanding their range steadily westward in the latter half of the twentieth century, thanks in large part to the spread of owl-friendly suburban habitat in the prairies and conifer forests of the Midwest and West. The owls arrived in western Washington in 1973. By 1975, they were breeding here, outcompeting the less aggressive and more specialized Spotted Owls. Now they are spreading into the deepest and most pristine parts of old growth forest, taking over the last fortress of the Spotted Owl's domain. And we humans, who facilitated the expansion of Barred Owls, are talking about hunting and killing them in order to save their endangered cousins. It's a controversial and poorly researched proposal, but it illustrates the kind of dilemmas we will face as global climate change and human development continue to alter the landscape of the wild.

Finding such a sublime creature in my favorite place on Earth should have produced unalloyed joy, a celebration of the pure glory of nature's creation. But how could I feel such joy when I could also see in my mind's eye a bird freighted with so much human baggage?

Barred Owls aren't the only birds that come to the Fill so burdened in my sight by ambiguity. Invasive European Starlings—for all their iridescent beauty—are harming native birds by taking over nest holes that are in short supply in urban habitats like the Fill. Human-fed Anna's Hummingbirds from California displace the smaller Rufous Hummingbirds that more truly belong in our lowlands and now come more rarely. Eurasian Collared-Doves, a cage bird that escaped into the wilds of California, has moved into our state and is breeding now with unknown impacts on our native doves. What's happy about any of these stories? Or any other stories about human impacts on the environment, not to mention human effects on other humans? As Eliphaz so deterministically tells Job, "Man is born unto trouble, as the sparks fly upward."

If this is true, why even bother to try to be happy? If the world is *supposed* to be full of woe because that's the way nature works, what good will it do to try to make the world better? Why not just resign ourselves to misery and plod through life with our heads hanging down, like Eeyore on a bad day? How can we live rejoicing amid suffering and pain?

Philosopher Huston Smith in his book *And Live Rejoicing* answers this question in the following way: "Happiness is the human birthright, and by extension we ought to cash in on that birthright and live rejoicing every day. We do this without denying...that sooner or later we all encounter tragedies that will beset us and show us that life is not a nonstop joyride.... Still, life's challenge is to make the joy an inclusive, all-embracing category that encompasses tragedy and transforms it."

I'm not sure I'm up to the task of embracing tragedy, nor any other nasty evils of the world. Embracing such things reminds me of the time my youngest son fell into University Slough. We were exploring the shore, and he got the idea it would be fun to walk on a small log projecting into the water. I think he may have been hoping to touch a dragonfly that had landed on the end of the log. His foot slipped and he plunged face-first into the rich stew of mud, goose poop, and other odoriferous biological residuum that edged the slough. My husband pulled him out, sputtering and crying, covered in goo from head to toe. "Here," said John, arms stiff as he held the screaming bundle out to me, "he needs a mother's comfort."

Gingerly, I took my smelly son into my arms and, breathing through my mouth, hugged him. I thus learned one *can* embrace the nether side of life, but it ain't pretty. We drove home with all the windows rolled down and me sitting on old newspapers. "That was cool," said my oldest son, through his nose.

Now, two decades later, we laugh at my reluctance to clutch my muddy child to my bosom. We have gained enough perspective to realize that many of the setbacks in life can be washed away by time, by love and acceptance, and most of all, by shared laughter. As Tevye sings in *Fiddler on the Roof*, "God would like us to be joyful even when our hearts lie panting on the floor." Or as my youngest son now says, "The comedy cat won't go in the tragedy bag."

Mel Birdsall has a different answer to the question of how to live rejoicing. Mel is the sunniest person I know. She's a young woman—only 29—who has already had her share of tribulation. But no matter how much trouble comes her way, she manages to sail through life with a smile. It's not because she is unaware of evil; she just chooses to look for something different in life. "I don't get bogged down by the sins of others," she says, "or my own. No matter what happens, there are good things to look forward to, to realize, and to see."

I like Mel's philosophy because it means you can separate into two parts the conundrum of how to feel joy in the presence of woe. First, there is the issue of being happy at any given moment. Second, there is the issue of fixing evil. Being happy in the moment is short term and achievable. Fixing evil is more of a long-term effort.

If, to be happy, you must wait until all the evil is fixed—until, for example, your job is totally fulfilling, your spouse is Sir Galahad only with more sex appeal, your kids are angels, your house is dust-free, and your lawn looks like a putting green—just when will that be? And how much power do you have to create that Eden on Earth?

If, on the other hand, you finally got that big project off your desk, your spouse took out the garbage without being asked, and your kids were polite in church, isn't that cause to rejoice? Even though such victories may be small, the happiness they bring can fill your entire soul with sunshine, like fresh-air molecules that fill every corner of your house when you open a window. As for the dust bunnies, weeds, and more fearsome creatures that still lurk in every spiritual corner, let's leave them be, at least for now. Instead, walk out the door, head for the Fill, and let nature's beauty shed its benedictions upon you.

We live with both ugliness and beauty, but we glory in the light.

Eight-spotted Skimmer © Dennis Paulson

32. Ripples

The armada of American Coots that occupies Union Bay each fall and winter has grown especially large this year. Seattle Audubon's Christmas Bird Count totted up 1,683 coots on December 29. Usually the coot fleet sails well out to sea, as it were, gathered in huge flotillas in the deeper water far from shore. The birds bunch together here for mutual protection against dive-bombing Bald Eagles, who prey on them.

When the eagles come, the coots squeeze themselves into a dense pack and begin to churn the water into a froth. The two white patches under the coots' tails and their bone-white bills create a confusing mix of flashes that are simply blinding against the dull black of their body feathers. An eagle trying to locate one coot in the scrum becomes so dazzled it cannot see straight. And so the coots are saved.

It is rare for the coot fleet to come close to shore. But on this cold day in late fall, the coots had dispersed across the small confines of Water Lily Cove near East Point. Many were foraging for water plants almost within touching distance from the shoreline, where I sat on my camp stool. The land here juts out into the cove, and I soon became surrounded by coots. It gave me a chance to study one of my favorite birds.

Mixed in with the coots were dozens of pinkish-brown American Wigeons. American Wigeons are dabbling ducks who associate with coots, probably because the wigeons like to steal the coots' food. Coots are not notable divers, but, unlike their ducky associates, they are willing to swim underwater for short periods to pull up plants from the lake bottom. After nabbing a tasty morsel, a coot pops up to the surface to eat its prize. That's when a waiting wigeon pounces, if ducks can be said to pounce.

The coots never seem to mourn the loss of their morsel. Maybe that's because they're magnanimous by nature, but I suspect it's really because they're too dumb to feel bad. As best as I can tell without actually measuring, a coot's head-to-body ratio appears to be one of the smallest in the animal kingdom. There just can't be too many brains in there. A coot who has been robbed paddles around for a while processing the event as if wondering where the food went, then shrugs it off and dives again.

Although I usually observe coots as a fleet rather than as a collection of individual vessels, every now and then one coot stands out from the crowd. Such was the case this day, when a juvenile came to forage among the Turtle Logs near me and unfortunately hopped up atop a loose log. Most of the Turtle Logs are firmly anchored by chains, mud, and vegetation, but this one log was a floater. When the coot got on, the log started to roll. The coot had to walk forward to stay on top. The log commenced to roll faster. The coot walked faster. The log began to spin. The coot began to run. Both whirled faster and faster until suddenly whoosh! The coot went flying off like an avian cannonball and landed with a giant splash among the lily pads. Baffled to find itself in water instead of on log, the coot looked around as if asking what had happened. "Don't look at me," I laughed. "I'm just as befuddled by the laws of physics as you are."

Watching the coots lead their little lives on the cove has made me appreciate the balance that exists within any species that both flocks and separates. Like us. We humans are social creatures who must flock together in community to be happy. Yet we are also individuals. Deep down, not a one of us thinks he or she is ordinary, whatever we may say publicly. Each of us is unique, and—dare I say?—special.

I do not think the coots find it difficult to strike a balance between individuality and community. They seem to flow without effort into and out of the flock. I suppose, given their small brain cases, they are guided by simple instinct.

Nothing about the way humans try to strike a similar balance is simple. On the contrary, our lives are filled with drama. When we're young, we obsess about who is dating whom, and for how long. We wonder what our peers think about our appearance. We worry whether we are progressing up the ladder of life with sufficient speed, and how high we are supposed to go to be called a success.

Now that I'm in my 60s, thank God, I don't worry about that adolescent stuff nearly as much as I used to, though I still sometimes wish I had straight hair instead of frizzy and could mix at parties without getting flop sweat.

But in addition to those remnant issues of who I think I am, and how I think I should fit in with others, now I also worry about how much of an effect my life here on Earth is having in the greater scheme of things. I can see that more of my life lies behind me than in front, so the amount of time I have to accomplish something meaningful keeps getting shorter. In addition, my competition keeps getting stiffer. In a world soon to be populated by 12 billion other people, how can any one individual hope to contribute anything worth remembering?

When I was a young writer working in the world of magazine publishing, I thought I would set the world on fire. Each month, a new issue of my magazine would come out, and I would ask myself: Did readers like what I had composed? Did my work help make their lives better? I wondered if my readers saved my creations, like people used to save old copies of *National Geographic,* bequeathing their wall of magazines in the garage to the next generation, who would add a new brick of their own every month.

"Well, I put my copy of our magazine in the bottom of my birdcage," a fellow staff writer told me one day. "The wood content of the paper makes it really absorbent. It's perfect."

Great. My best creative efforts sentenced to collecting bird poop. I guess I felt glad that my writing continued to serve a useful purpose after it was read, but somehow I had had something more archival in mind. I learned about the fate of my magazine articles about the same time businesswoman Leona Helmsley, the Queen of Mean,

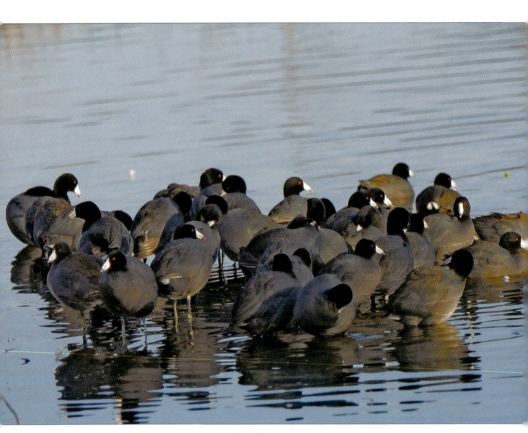

American Coots © Doug Parrott

famously said, "Only the little people pay taxes." Right. I definitely pay taxes. Thus, between the bird poop and the business pap, the conclusion was inescapable. I am one of the little people.

Mostly, I'm glad to be small. For one thing, like a lot of other folks, I dislike looking at images of myself. Imagine, if you were famous, how you'd squirm every time your pores, each the size of a fish platter, flashed on the big screen at your local movie theater. But the real reason I like being counted among the vast flotilla of ordinary people is the feeling I get knowing I am part of a species that accomplishes big things because of the little efforts contributed by each one of us. It means that we can each make a big difference in our own small way. We can all smile at a passer-by, compliment a sales clerk, or pick up something an elderly person has dropped.

We never know, when we perform these acts of kindness, what effect they might have. I suppose usually the recipient feels a brief spurt of joy, then forgets about it. But every now and then, an act of kindness makes a deep impact, sending out ripples in all directions,

American Wigeon © Doug Schurman

touching people we never knew, changing lives, changing worlds.

One incident in my husband's life has certainly done this for me. Dr. Doug Harryman was an orthopaedic surgeon on the faculty of the University of Washington. He was also my husband John's best friend. Tragically, Doug developed bone cancer in his 40s. For many months, Doug continued to practice surgery and to teach his students, even though pain and chemotherapy wracked his spirit and weakened his body. One day, Doug was speaking to his chairman, Dr. Rick Matsen. They were on the tenth floor of the UW Medical Center, where the Orthopaedics Department offices were located. Suddenly, while Doug was talking, his head slumped forward.

"Are you all right?" Rick asked him.

"Rick, I can't move," said Doug, and Rick realized his friend was dying. Doug's blood count was too low, and he needed a transfusion instantly. Without wasting a moment, Rick gathered Doug up into his arms and ran with him down ten flights of stairs to the emergency room, for Rick was strong, and Doug had become light.

Rick saved Doug's life that day. In so doing, he also gave my husband a profound lesson about the humanity and sacrifice common in medicine. John saw the way Rick practiced these ideals and has long admired how he has imparted these beliefs to young doctors.

My husband does not tell this story very often because he chokes up whenever he tries, but he has managed to tell it to me. The story of Rick's act has in turn inspired me. In dark times, when I despair because of human beings' cruelty to each other and to the Earth we all share, I call to mind this story, and I remember that we have within ourselves good angels, too.

Now I give this story to you, in the hope that you too will be inspired to remember those angels. I tell you this story for another reason: Because I know that each of you has already performed many acts of bravery and kindness. I know you have already inspired other people by your example, whether you realize it or not. I know that although we exist as individuals, we build as community. And I know whatever you add to your community makes the world better.

You do matter.

Part V
Appendices

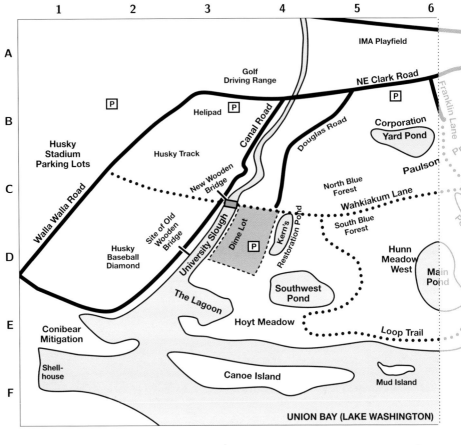

Alder Grove	C7	Helipad	B3
Boy Scout Pond	D8	Hoyt Meadow	E4
Canal Road	B4	Hunn Meadow East	E7
Canoe Island	F4	Hunn Meadow West	D5
Carp Pond (see Southwest Pond)		Husky Baseball Diamond	D2
Central Pond (see Main Pond)		Husky Stadium Parking Lots	B1
Conibear Mitigation	E1	Husky Track	B2
Corporation Yard Pond	B6	IMA Playfield	A5
CUH (Center for Urban Horticulture) Buildings	C8	Kern's Restoration Pond	D4
		The Lagoon	E3
Dime Lot (also E5 Lot)	D4	Lake Washington (Union Bay)	F5
Douglas Road	B5	Leaky Pond	C7
E5 Lot (see Dime Lot)		Lone Pine Tree (now burned)	D7
East Basin (see Yesler Swamp)		Loop Trail	D7, E5
East Point	E9	Main Pond (also Central Pond)	D6
Franklin Lane	B6	Mary Gates Memorial Dr. NE	B7
Golf Driving Range	A4	Mud Island	F5
Greenhouses	C9	NE Clark Road	A5

202

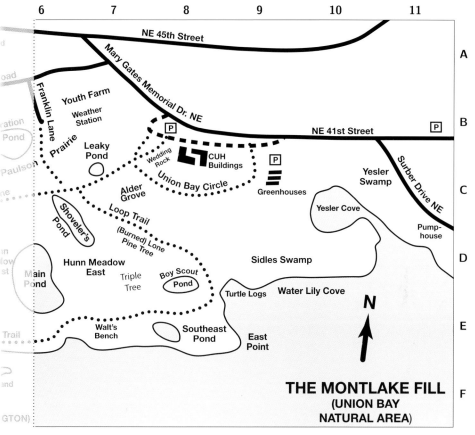

THE MONTLAKE FILL
(UNION BAY NATURAL AREA)

NE 41st Street	B10	Surber Drive NE		C11
NE 45th Street	A8	Surber Grove (see Yesler Swamp)		
New Wooden Bridge	C3	Triple Tree		E7
North Blue Forest	C5	Turtle Logs		E9
Old Wooden Bridge	D3	Union Bay (Lake Washington)		F5
(now gone; only pylons remain)		Union Bay Circle		C8
Paulson Prairie	C6	University Slough		D3
Pumphouse	D11	Wahkiakum Lane		C5
Reading Rocks (see Walt's Bench)	E7	Walla Walla Road		D1
Shellhouse	F1	Walt's Bench (also Reading Rocks)		E7
Shoveler's Pond	C6	Water Lily Cove (also The Cove)		
Sidles Swamp	D9	Weather Station		B7
South Blue Forest	D5	Wedding Rock		C8
Southeast Pond	E8	Yesler Cove		C10
Southwest Pond	D4	Yesler Swamp (also Surber Grove)		C10
(also Carp Pond)		Youth Farm (née Youth Garden)		B7

A. The Meaning of the Fill

Montlake Fill was made for artists. Not on purpose, of course. Originally, it was a lake created by the glaciers that ground their way down from the Far North during the last Ice Age. After the ice melted, the lake lay undisturbed for 10,000 years. Then we humans decided to re-engineer it in 1916 so that it connected to saltwater. We lowered the lake by eight or nine feet and brought forth wetlands. Nature went to work on the new land, seeding it with marsh plants that attracted wildlife. Then we humans stepped in again, exiling nature in 1921 to make way for a garbage dump. Again, nature went to work, bringing life to the barren dirt that covered the landfill cribs as they closed, one by one, each filled to the brim with garbage. Now, the Fill is a "natural area," specifically, Union Bay Natural Area. Meaning what, exactly?

Only the artists can tell us. That's because, above all else, the Fill is the intersection of wild nature and human nature. It is a little piece of habitat in the heart of a city, where some 255 different species of birds find refuge, where otters play, and beavers build their lodges. No one manages their activities, for the Fill is not a zoo. It *is* owned, however—owned by people who sometimes want to mold it to suit their purposes. Hence the intersection.

Intersection sounds so benign, doesn't it? A gentle coming together, perhaps, as when two friends meet. Or maybe a crossroads, where different paths encounter each other and offer choices to the traveler. But intersection is far from benign. Originally, the word came from the Latin *intersecare*, meaning to cut asunder. We and the wild are not in union anymore. We are disconnected.

In fact, ever since the first cave person told his or her spouse, "Do we have to eat raw meat *again*??" and the spouse, in exasperation, threw the chops into a convenient fire, thus inventing haute cuisine, we have distanced ourselves from the wild. We invented electricity and made day into night. We invented heating and air conditioning and eliminated the seasons. We kill the big predators and spray the little ones. We build machines to enhance our physical gifts. We can go faster than any animal, fly higher, see further, eat better.

But no matter how far away we get from the dirt and danger of the wild, we still live within nature because we live on Planet Earth, and the planet is governed by nature. We cannot cut ourselves off from it, though the separation now is great. Artists are the ones who can bridge those two worlds and knit together what was cut apart.

Lisa Ravenholt is one such artist. In March, she brought her dance group to the Fill to perform a dance she had choreographed based on the birds she observed here. Her dance group are elders from Ballard Landmark—a GenCare Lifestyle Community for retirees—and they specialize in seated-dancing. They walked out to Walt Williams's memorial bench to perform "Flight." Walt was a long-time Fill regular, a beloved birder whose ashes lie in Union Bay. His wife, Jackie, was on hand to watch the performance. As the music played and the elders danced, a Great Blue Heron rose into the air and floated away. Dancers and nature began to merge. Each dancer's face became an entry to the soul within, the humanity of each woman's life a history for all to read. As the dancers froze into a last pose, I glanced over at Jackie. Tears were falling from her eyes. "Walt would have loved this," she whispered.

I know. Just as the other artists on these pages know. May their inspiration bring you peace and joy.

Red-necked Phalarope on Main Pond © Kathrine Lloyd

"Flight," a dance performed at the Fill, choreographed by Lisa Ravenholt. Dancers pictured (clockwise from top left): LuElla Heitzman, Geraldine Wallace, Bernice Olliver, Clineene Smith, Shirley Monson, Barbara A. Bowen, and Ethel Hamilton. Photograph © Thomas Schworer

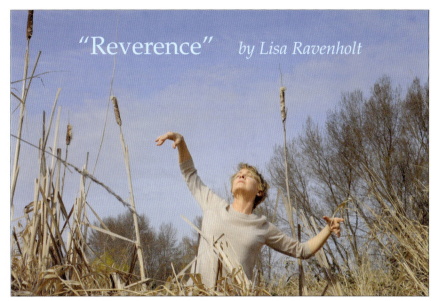

Ravenholt performing "Reverence" at the Fill. Photograph © Thomas Schworer

I believe we are hardwired at our most basic animal level to express ourselves through dance. As a species, we rely on body language to illuminate our understanding of the meaning behind words. Wittingly or not, we all speak the language of movement.

As a choreographer, I practice and create dance in a field of awareness. I go to my senses. I feel things. I open and listen to my surroundings, observing what wants to move through me like the weather. From attention and stillness I find movement. I empty to fill. In this way, my creative process begins when I step mindfully into the moment. This can happen anywhere, but it happens consistently when I enter the beauty that lives in Montlake Fill.

How do I translate nature's expression into movement? It may come from the architecture of a certain plant, the spatial dynamism of a whole landscape, the hunting movement phrase of a heron, the rhythm of a bird's call, or the snap of a storm-broken tree limb. Whatever grabs my attention, it becomes like a fly hitting a spider's web—something trips a vibratory response in me and triggers a desire to move and create. In this manner, phrases often tumble out from seemingly random inspirations, and I feed my soul.

Creativity and nature are wild things. When I step into nature, I come into the source of my own true nature—I am danced by nature, the great humanizing mediator for the wild in us all.

Turkey Vulture number story © Ethan Madsen

When grandparents David and Lois Madsen forwarded Connie Sidles's Montlake Fill story about Turkey Vultures to their grandson Ethan Madsen in California, Ethan remembered seeing vultures on a trip to Alaska. He was inspired to write and draw this number story: "There were 3 hungry Turkey Vultures. They found 3 dead porcupines hit by a car. So they all had dinner. 3 + 3 = 6."

The Meaning of the Fill

Main Pond in summer ©Mary Lou Smith

Common Yellowthroat © Alexandra MacKenzie

The Meaning of the Fill

Wood Duck © Molly Hashimoto

Shoveler's Pond, Winter ©Sarah T. Yeager

The Meaning of the Fill

Dragonfly © Hiroko Seki

Buffleheads at Montlake Fill © Tony Parr

A Bald Eagle attempts to steal an Osprey's catch above Union Bay © Jane Sandes

Shoveler's Pond ©Suzanne E. Peterson

Hope in a Blue Egg
by Judith Yarrow

A Sunday walk along the lake,
the usual spring floaters—buffleheads,
wigeons, gadwalls, and scaups.
And one Pied-billed Grebe couple

circling last year's nesting spot
among the lily pads. But the beavers
had cleared away the lily plants.
Now where would they nest?

One day I'd seen a grebe there,
nestled on a pile of decaying
water plants—stems, mud, leaves.
Through the willows along the shore,

I spied on her. Back to me, she
stood up and just like that
popped out a tiny, blue egg
from her little blunt-tailed behind.

Grebe nests constantly fall apart.
Brooding grebes add to their nests
—lily stems, pond weed, milfoil—
until their babies fledge. And then the nest

rots away. The young grebes haunt
the spot, until one day they, too, are gone,
but remember the place and return,
led by old memories to a new season.

Turning Green

by Rachel Sprague

White apple blossoms welcome me
in to fill my pockets with treasure.
The wind strokes the grass
and the sound transforms me
into the green I see.
Electricity runs through my fingers
into the ground.
The sapphire blue lake
fills my gourd with peace.
Like a bird surrounded by leaves to
block the wind
I feel safe at home.

The Meaning of the Fill

Union Bay Natural Area ©Carleen Ormbrek Zimmerman

Carleen Ormbrek Zimmerman belongs to a group of artists called the Urban Sketchers. Their manifesto says: "1. We draw on location, indoors or out, capturing what we see from direct observation. 2. Our drawings tell the story of our surroundings, the places we live and where we travel. 3. Our drawings are a record of time and place. 4. We are truthful to the scenes we witness. 5. We use any kind of media and cherish our individual styles. 6. We support each other and draw together. 7. We share our drawings online. 8. We show the world, one drawing at a time."

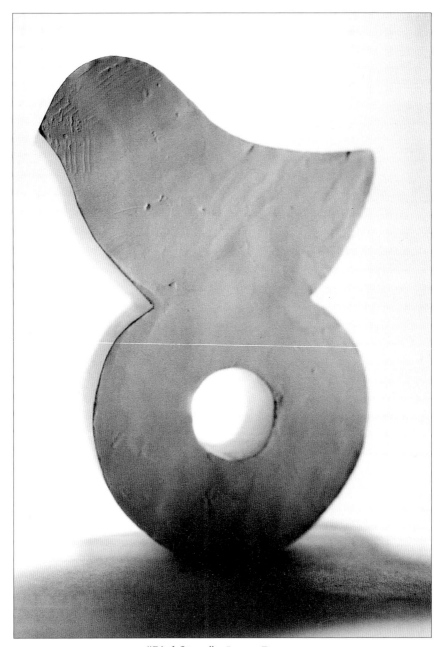

"Bird Stone" © James Brems

B. Birds of Montlake Fill

Just when you think every bird that *could* be found at Montlake Fill *has* been found, a new rarity shows up that makes your jaw drop. Birds do fly, after all, and the winds can help them wend their way almost anywhere as long as they have sufficient food, water, rest, safe havens from predators, and the desire to wander.

The following list originally appeared in *In My Nature* in 2009. It was updated in *Second Nature* in 2011. Since then, the Fill has hosted six new rarities never seen here before since record-keeping began in the 1890s: Barred Owl, Alder Flycatcher, Eastern Phoebe, Black-billed Magpie, Townsend's Solitaire, and McCown's Longspur. In addition, two new species have been included from older records left out in earlier books: Ross's Goose and American White Pelican.

The list has been compiled with the help of numerous birders over the years (see the list of contributors at the end). Despite the great care we have all taken to be complete and accurate, mistakes might have been made (as the politicians say). I encourage readers to contact me with additional sightings and/or corrections.

The total number of bird species ever seen at the Fill is now 255.

GREATER WHITE-FRONTED GOOSE Uncommon winter resident. More common as migrant. High count: Fifty flying over, May 4, 2010 (*CSi*).
EMPEROR GOOSE Rare visitor. One August 1988 (*KA*).
SNOW GOOSE Occasional winter resident; uncommon spring migrant. High count: 200 flying over, October 8, 2007 (*CSi*). Unusually late spring sighting: One May 4 through 9, 2013 (*CSi*).
ROSS'S GOOSE One April 24, 1990 (*EN*).
BRANT Rare visitor. One for half a day, late March 1986 (*KA*).
CACKLING GOOSE Uncommon winter visitor and migrant, sometimes in large flocks.
CANADA GOOSE Common resident and breeder.

Canvasback © Doug Parrott

Birds of Montlake Fill

MUTE SWAN Occasional introduced resident and breeder. Three May 15, 1980; three September 29 and November 1, 1980; two December 11, 1980; two with young May 27, 1982; four December 27, 1982; one April 8, 1983; two with young June 11, 1983 (*ER*). Two attempted to nest, July 1989 (*CSi*). A pair with two young July 16, 1995 (*DP*). Latest sighting: One December 17, 1998 (*WOS/TAv*).

TRUMPETER SWAN Formerly rare winter visitor; now regular after the winter of 2008-2009, when eleven (including three juveniles) overwintered. High count: Eighteen on January 2 and 6, 2012 (*CSi*).

TUNDRA SWAN Rare winter visitor. Reported in the 1940s (*HL*). One late October through mid-November 1970 (*FK*). Three December 17, 1998 (*WOS/TAv*). One near shellhouse December 22, 2008; twenty flying over, March 6, 2010 (*CSi*). One arriving December 21, 2011 and overwintering (*EvH, CSi*). One arriving December 8, then three arriving December 30, 2012 and overwintering (*EvH, CSi*).

WOOD DUCK Common (though sometimes reclusive) resident and breeder. Bred more commonly in the 1940s (*HL*), diminished after habitat loss, now common again as swampy woodlands increase. Unusual sighting: Mother with nine babies May 28, 2006 (*CSi*).

GADWALL Common resident and breeder.

EURASIAN WIGEON Uncommon winter resident. Usually one or two present each year.

AMERICAN WIGEON Common winter resident, rare in summer.

AMERICAN BLACK DUCK Rare introduced visitor. Two separate birds in molt, late 1970s, late summer, staying for some months (*KA*). One male December 29, 1979 through June 10, 1980; one male November 7, 1981 (*ER*).

MALLARD Common resident and breeder.

BLUE-WINGED TEAL Uncommon but regular spring and summer visitor.

CINNAMON TEAL Common summer resident and breeder. Occasional winter resident.

NORTHERN SHOVELER Common winter resident and sometime summer breeder. Most recent breeding record: spring 2011 (*KL*).

NORTHERN PINTAIL Uncommon visitor, sometime winter resident; recorded every month (*ER, CSi*).

GREEN-WINGED TEAL Common winter resident, returning by late July (*BtW*). Occasional summer resident (*ER*). Eurasian subspecies (Common Teal) is a rare winter visitor: One between January 27 and April 27, 2000 (*CSi*). One January 4 to May 7, 2001 (*BV; WOS/TAv, JB*). One January 11, 2004 (*SMa*). One arrived January 29, 2010 and stayed some months (*CSi and many observers*). Probably same individual returned December 5, 2010 and stayed until April 26, 2011 (*CSi and many observers*).

CANVASBACK Uncommon winter resident.

REDHEAD Found regularly in the fall (usually most common in November) during the early 1970s (*ER, DP*). Now uncommon visitor in winter or spring; usually an individual or a small flock is present every year.

TUFTED DUCK Rare visitor. One May 3, 1996 (*WOS/JHe*). One February 3 to 12, 2012 (*CSi, MVe*); and again April 13, 2012 (*KaS*).

RING-NECKED DUCK Common winter resident.

GREATER SCAUP Common winter resident.

LESSER SCAUP Common winter resident.

SURF SCOTER Rare visitor. One adult male February 11, 1980; one immature male October 7, 1980 (*ER*). One immature October 8, 2009 (*EvH*).

WHITE-WINGED SCOTER Rare visitor. Nine September 22, 1939 (*MC*).

LONG-TAILED DUCK Rare visitor. One March 26, 1981 (*ER*). One March 4, 1990 (*DP*). One October 29, 2006 (*WOS/JBr*).

BUFFLEHEAD Common winter resident. Occasionally one stays through the summer.

COMMON GOLDENEYE   Uncommon winter resident and rare summer visitor. Two records for June: one in 1981, one in 1983 (*ER*).
BARROW'S GOLDENEYE   Rare visitor. One January 21, 1981 (*ER*). Two April 25, 1988 (*KA*). One February 21, 2007 (*BtW*). One December 31, 2009 (*AdS*). One male February 5, 2012, seen off and on with a second male through March 11, 2012; one male with female March 25, 2012 (*CSi*.) One first-year male May 12, 2012 (*EvH*).
HOODED MERGANSER   Common winter resident and uncommon summer breeder.
COMMON MERGANSER   Common winter resident and abundant spring migrant, as large numbers stage in the lake and bay before migrating.
RED-BREASTED MERGANSER   Rare visitor. More common in the 1940s in the fall (*HL*). Five in April 1982 (*ER*). One April 15, 2008; two April 19, 2009 (*CSi*). Two October 8, 2009 (*EvH*). One November 4, 2012; one January 10, 2013 (*CSi*).
RUDDY DUCK   Uncommon winter resident, formerly abundant: 500 January 1983 (*ER*). Rare summer visitor: one July 5 to 26, 1980; one August 19 to 29, 1980; three August 5, 1982; one August 12, 1982 (*ER*). Successful nesting 1987 through 1989 (*KA*). One July 25 through September 18, 2008; one June 28, 2012 (*CSi*). Unusually high count: Seventeen on October 5, 2012 (*KaS*).
RING-NECKED PHEASANT   Formerly common resident and breeder, now extirpated. Last reported: One vocalizing July 12, 2009 (*GOO*). One seen near Yesler Swamp July 21, 2009 (*MaH*).
CALIFORNIA QUAIL   Formerly common resident and breeder, now extirpated, although rare visitors still appear occasionally. Most recent sightings: One April 8, 2009 (*DPa*). One calling May 5 through 9, 2009; one February 2 and 19, 2010; one February 26, 2012 (*CSi*). One May 26, 2012 (*GP*).
NORTHERN BOBWHITE   Rare visitor. One September 11, 1997 (*WOS/TAv*).
COMMON LOON   Rare visitor. Reported regularly in the winter in the 1940s (*HL*). One flyover July 16, 1980; one in Union Bay April 17, 1982 (*ER*). One flyover April 16, 2008 (*WOS/TAv*). One in Union Bay October 30, 2008; one July 28, 2012 (*CSi*). One September 15, 2012 (*MSc, EmR*). One April 21, 2013 (*EvH*).
RED-THROATED LOON   One March 20,1943 (*ER*). Occasional winter visitor (*DP*).
PIED-BILLED GREBE   Common resident and breeder.
HORNED GREBE   Uncommon winter resident.
RED-NECKED GREBE   Rare visitor. One November 1979; one June 7, 1982 (*ER*). Since 2007, at least one present every fall or winter. Most recent sightings: One in breeding plumage April 30, 2011 (*CSi*). One July 3, 2011 (*WW*). One August 27, 2011; one April 7, 2012 (*CSi*).
EARED GREBE   Rare visitor. More common in the 1940s, arriving in fall (*HL*). Occasional winter visitor in 1970s (*FK*). One February 28, 1981 (*ER*). Two October 28, 1986; one September 18, 1989 (*KA*). One September 19, 2009 (*AlG*). One October 29 and 31, 2011 (*EvH, CSi, AlG*). One November 28, 2011 (*RyM*). One September 25, 2012 (*CSi*).
WESTERN GREBE   Uncommon winter visitor and migrant. Unusually high count: Three on October 16, 2012 (*CSi*).
CLARK'S GREBE   Rare visitor. Two calling July 21, 1989 (*KA*).
AMERICAN WHITE PELICAN   Rare visitor. One November 22, 1992 (*RY*).
DOUBLE-CRESTED CORMORANT   Common winter resident.
AMERICAN BITTERN   Former uncommon resident and breeder (*HL*), now scarce. Most recent sightings: One September 11, 2006 (*MtB*). One February 4, 2007; one October 5, 2007 (*BtW*). One July 25, 2008 (*CSi*). One July 7, 2009 (*KL*). One August 17, 2009; one August 31 to September 6, 2011; one August 11, 2012 (*CSi*).
GREAT BLUE HERON   Common resident and occasional breeder. Successful nesting in 1989 (*KA*). New heronry established on UW campus (four nests) near Drumheller Fountain

2008; forty-one nests reported in 2012 (*PCa*). High count: Fifty-three birds on Dempsey Gym roof, March 1, 2012 (*CSi*).

GREAT EGRET   Rare visitor. One June 16 to July 2, 1987 (*KA*). Two May 15, 2000 (*WOS/RR*).

CATTLE EGRET   Rare late fall or winter visitor. One November 22 through December 25, 1989 (also noted in Ballard) (*RD*, *KB*, *FB*). One November 11 through 18, 2004 (*WOS/FB*, *KAn*; *MtB*, *CSi*). One November 5 through 9, 2007 (*BtW*; *WOS/NLr*, *CSi*, *CPe*).

GREEN HERON   Uncommon summer resident and breeder. First state nesting record, 1939 (*HL*).

BLACK-CROWNED NIGHT-HERON   Rare visitor. Two reported in the 1940s (*HL*). One December 5, 1974 (*FK*). One December 10, 1975 (fide *EH*). One November 20, 1976 through January 8, 1977 (fide *EH*). One August 15 to September 3, 1987 (*KA*).

TURKEY VULTURE   Uncommon spring and fall migrant, only flyovers; not reported every year. Most recent sightings: Eighteen September 26, 2008; two April 8, 2009 (*CSi*). Two April 2, 2011 (*PDu*, *WW*). One June 7, 2011; one March 7, 2012; six September 29, 2012 (*CSi*).

OSPREY   Uncommon summer visitor. A few come by regularly in summer and stay briefly to catch fish.

GOLDEN EAGLE   Rare visitor. One March 21, 2010 (*CSi*).

BALD EAGLE   Common resident and breeder. Current nest on Talaris site nearby; another nest near Broadmoor.

NORTHERN HARRIER   Common visitor in the 1940s (*HL*); only single visitors now, mostly in fall, although reported every year.

SHARP-SHINNED HAWK   Occasional visitor, more common as fall migrant or in winter. Most recent records: One January 5, 2011; one October 27, 2011; one January 19, 2012; one February 7, 2012; one off and on from October 5 through December 8, 2012; one January 2 and 3, 2013 (*CSi*). One March 17, 2013 (*AlG*). One April 20, 2013 (*CSi*).

COOPER'S HAWK   Common visitor in small numbers.

NORTHERN GOSHAWK   Rare winter visitor. One February 3 and 19, 1972 (*FK*). Several sightings in winter of 1981 to 1982 (*ER*).

RED-SHOULDERED HAWK   Rare visitor. One August 7, 2006 (*CCx*). One February 5, 2010; one March 30, 2013 (*CSi*).

RED-TAILED HAWK   One to three usually present in spring, fall, and winter. One pair year-round resident in 2008 (*CSi*).

ROUGH-LEGGED HAWK   Rare visitor. Two flew over in late October 1974 (*KA*). One February 3, 1982 (*ER*).

AMERICAN KESTREL   Formerly regular fall visitor (*KA*), now rare. Most recent sightings: One September 27, 2009 (*HG*, *HN*). One September 11, 2010; one April 4, 2011 (*CSi*). One October 2, 2011 (*HG*). One March 10, 18, and 20, 2012 (*CSi*). One November 18, 2012 (*BMc*).

MERLIN   Uncommon visitor year-round.

PEREGRINE FALCON   Uncommon but regular visitor year-round.

VIRGINIA RAIL   Common year-round resident and breeder, more easily heard than seen. At least nine pairs nested in various ponds, coves, and shoreline cattails in 2012 and 2013 (*CSi*). High count: Seven babies in University Slough June 16, 2013 (*AmD*).

SORA   Uncommon summer resident and breeder, becoming almost rare now. Most recent sightings: One May 26, 2010 (*EvH*). One August 28, 2010 (*JTb and many observers*). One September 7 and 10, 2010 (*CSi*, *KAS*). One April 23, 2011 (*KAS*, *HG*, *HN*). One May 1, 2011 (*CSi*). One juvenile August 20, 2011 (*TK*). One May 9, 2012 (*AM*). One September 23, 2012 (*TK*). Extremely rare winter record: One January 17, 2013 (*CSi*, *BlB*).

AMERICAN COOT   Common resident and rare breeder.

SANDHILL CRANE   Rare visitor, only flyovers. Two October 12, 1980 (**ER**). Three September 17, 2007 (**WOS/BtW**). One September 27, 2009 (**EvH**). One May 27, 2012 (**PCa, JB, DH**).
BLACK-BELLIED PLOVER   Regular migrant in 1940s (**HL**). Now rare. Two May 14, 1979; one May 5, 1980, one April 6 and 9, 1983; one August 1 and 8, 1983; one first week of September 1983 (**ER**). One September 12, 1985 (**KA**). One April 22, 2004 (**WOS/EH**).
AMERICAN GOLDEN-PLOVER   Rare migrant. One September 14, 1981 (**DP**).
SEMIPALMATED PLOVER   Rare migrant. High count: Five on May 13, 1986 (**KA**). One May 31, 1996; one July 17, 1997 (**CM**). One August 6, 2000 (**WOS/JB**). Three August 7, 2000 (**CSi**). One April 29, 2007 (**WOS/MEg, PC**). One May 8, 2008 (**BV**).
KILLDEER   Common resident and breeder.
BLACK-NECKED STILT   Rare migrant. One May 12, 1988 (**KA**). One April 29, 1993 (**WOS/TB**).
AMERICAN AVOCET   Rare migrant. One May 28, 1980 (**ER**). One March 31, 1988 (**KA**). One May 30, 1998 (**WOS/BB**).
SPOTTED SANDPIPER   Uncommon resident and regular migrant. Bred commonly in the 1940s (**HL**) and annually in the 1970s (**KA**). Last reported nesting: 1987 (**KA**).
SOLITARY SANDPIPER   Uncommon spring and fall migrant; usually one present briefly each year. Most recent sightings: Three May 10, 2011 (**CSi**). Two August 16 and 17, 2012 (**DPa, CSi**). One May 4 and another May 19, 2013 (**CSi**).
GREATER YELLOWLEGS   Occasional spring migrant, uncommon fall migrant.
LESSER YELLOWLEGS   Occasional spring migrant, uncommon fall migrant.
UPLAND SANDPIPER   Rare migrant. One August 18, 1998 (**WOS/TAv**).
WHIMBREL   Rare visitor. One May 4, 1974 (**FK**). One in late September 1975 (**KA**). One May 3, 1981 (**ER**). One April 30, 1994 (**WOS/DMc**).
SANDERLING   Rare migrant. Two juveniles September 25, 1986 (**KA**).
SEMIPALMATED SANDPIPER   Formerly uncommon but regular fall migrant, now rare. Six spring records: One May 25, 1974 (**FK**). One May 13, 1976 (**DP**). One May 8, 1982 (**ER**). One May 10 to 12, 1996 (**CM; WOS/JiF**). One May 10, 2000 (**WOS/TAv**). Most recent fall records: One July 22, 2008 (**EvH**). One July 23, 2010 (**EvH, KAS**). One August 15, 2010 (**CSi, DPa**). One August 8, 2011 (**CSi**). One July 16 and 17, 2012 (**CSi, BlB**).
WESTERN SANDPIPER   Uncommon spring and fall migrant, becoming rarer as Main Pond gets woodier.
LEAST SANDPIPER   Common spring and fall migrant, becoming more uncommon as Main Pond gets woodier. Rare winter visitor: one January 9, 1982; one February 5 through 9, 1982 (**ER**).
BAIRD'S SANDPIPER   Rare fall migrant. Highest count: Three on September 10, 1989 (**KA**). One spring record: May 9, 1985 (**KA**). Most recent sightings: August 14, 2007 (**CSi**); August 15 and 19, 2007 (**BtW**).
PECTORAL SANDPIPER   Rare spring and fall migrant, although usually at least one is present briefly each year. Slightly more common in fall than in spring. Most recent sightings: One July 22, 2008 (**EvH**). One May 15, 2009 (**CSi**). One September 12 and 13, 2010 (**CSi, TK, KAS**). Four May 18, 2012 (**DSu**); three still present May 19, 2012 (**CSi**). One September 25 to 29, 2012 (**CSi, SR**).
SHARP-TAILED SANDPIPER   Rare migrant. One September 12, 1987 (**MEg**). One September 29, 1996 (**WOS/KA**), last seen October 14, 1996 (**CM**).
DUNLIN   Occasional winter visitor, occasional spring migrant. High count: More than forty on November 5, 2006 (**CSi**).
RUFF   Rare visitor. One September 1, 1995 (**WOS/RSt**).
STILT SANDPIPER   Rare visitor. One July 29, 1965 (**FK**). One August 30 to September 8, 1981 (**ER**). Two September 13, 1981 (**EH**). One August 29, 1989 (**KA**). One August 31 to September 1, 1996 (**CM, CSi**). One August 17 and 18, 1997 (**CM, BV**).

Dunlin © Doug Parrott

BUFF-BREASTED SANDPIPER Rare visitor. One stayed seven days, reported in the 1940s (*HL*).
SHORT-BILLED DOWITCHER Rare migrant. One July 24, 2007 (*CSi*).
LONG-BILLED DOWITCHER Uncommon spring migrant, common fall migrant.
WILSON'S SNIPE Uncommon fall, winter, and spring resident.
WILSON'S PHALAROPE Formerly uncommon spring migrant now becoming more rare. One fall record: August 1, 1987 (*KA*). High counts: Four on June 5, 2003 (*WOS/MtB*). One female, two males May 24, 2008 (*CSi*). Most recent sighting: One June 10, 2011 (*WW*).
RED-NECKED PHALAROPE Rare migrant. More common in the 1940s (*HL*). High count: Sixty-five on May 20, 1980 (*ER*). Most recent records: One August 9, 2009 (*EvH*). One to four August 20 to 23, 2009 (*KL, CSi, and many observers*). One August 11, 2010 (*DPa, CSi*).
BONAPARTE'S GULL Formerly common spring and fall migrant, now rare. Most recent sightings: One November 11, 2010 (*JeB*). One November 16, 2010; one in breeding plumage April 24, 2011; one in breeding plumage July 15, 2012 (*CSi*).
BLACK-HEADED GULL Rare visitor. One April 19, 1998 (*SMa, CSi*).
FRANKLIN'S GULL One reported in the 1940s (*HL*) for first county record. Occasional in fall (*DP*). Most recent sighting: one August 29, 2009 (*EvH*).
MEW GULL Common fall and winter visitor.
RING-BILLED GULL Common winter resident, less common in summer.
WESTERN GULL Uncommon winter visitor; usually one present each year. Most recent sightings: One January 26, 2011; one February 26, 2011; one January 10 to 21, 2012; one January 20, 2013 (*CSi*).
CALIFORNIA GULL Uncommon but regular fall and winter visitor.
HERRING GULL Uncommon but regular fall and winter visitor.
THAYER'S GULL Uncommon but regular fall and winter visitor.
GLAUCOUS-WINGED GULL Common resident. Nested in summers of 1984 and 1985 (*ER*).
CASPIAN TERN Uncommon summer visitor, though present every summer.
BLACK TERN Rare visitor. One August 22, 1972 (*FK*). Two May 28, 1975; one late May 1976; one early June 1977 (*KA*). One June 8, 1980 (*ER*). One May 14, 2000 (*CSi*).
COMMON TERN Rare fall migrant. Eighteen August 19, 1980; two September 2, 1980; 25 September 13, 1982 (*ER*). Flock of 37 September 2, 1985; another flock of 26 September 3, 1989 (*KA*). Three September 10, 2003 (*WOS/SMa*).
ROCK PIGEON Common resident in University Village, commonly seen as flyovers and as foragers in playfields and in burns.
BAND-TAILED PIGEON Uncommon resident in the 1980s (*DP*), now uncommon visitor. Possible nesting: May 2009; June 2013 (*CSi*).
EURASIAN COLLARED-DOVE First one May 10, 2008 (*CSi*); one or two seen each year thereafter (*GOO, CSi*); becoming regular as of 2012 (*CSi*).
MOURNING DOVE Uncommon visitor that can appear in any season; usually one present each year.
BARN OWL Rare visitor. One October 1972 (*KA*). One September 4 and 16, 1980; one March 26, 1981; two May 4, 1981 (*ER*). One seen regularly in late July 2008 (*CSi*). One October 9, 2008 (*MtB*). One August 16, 2009 (*DPa, KAS, HG, HN*). One September 12, 2009 (*CSi and many observers*).
SHORT-EARED OWL Occasional visitor, now rare. One November 1992; one November 1995; one October 1996 (*BV*). One October 13, 1997 (*WOS/TAv*). One November 8, 1999 (*WOS/ED*). One October 19, 2006 (*BtW*). One November 25, 2006 (*WOS/TAv*). One January 17, 2007 (*BtW*). One November 13, 2008 (*EvH*). One October 23 and 24, 2011 (*WW, FR*). One February 2, 2012; one June 8, 2012 (*EDo*). One August 10, 2012 (*CSi*).

GREAT HORNED OWL   Rare visitor. One March 18, 2007 (*MFM, CSi*). One November 7, 2007 (*MtB, TM*).
BARRED OWL   Rare visitor, probably soon to become resident. One October 23, 2011 (*WW, CSi*). One off and on from September 2 to 27, 2012 (*MM, CSi, and many observers*). One June 2, 2013 (*JA, TL*).
SNOWY OWL   Rare visitor. Two wintered in 1973 to 1974 (*FK*). One seen in winter of 1975 to 1976 and 1977 to 1978 (*KA*). One March 3 to 9, 1979 (*ER*). One December 11, 2005 (*WOS/MtD*).
NORTHERN SAW-WHET OWL   Rare visitor. One October 14, 1995 (*WOS/PHa*). One November 28 through December 3, 2009 (*KAS, CSi, JAS, and many observers*). One October 17, 2012 (*KM*).
COMMON NIGHTHAWK   Common summer resident in the 1940s (*HL*). Nesting reported in the early 1970s (*FK*). Now rare migrant. One June 3, 1988 (*KA*). One September 20, 2002 (*WOS/SMa*). One August 27, 2004 (*WOS/SMa*). One September 18 and 19, 2006 (*WOS/PCr; EvH*). One June 8, 2008 (*MtB*). One September 11, 2010 (*CSi*). One June 9, 2012 (*KP*). One June 14, 2012 (*BlB*).
COMMON POORWILL   Rare visitor. One May 20 to 25, 2006 (*WOS/LKi, AdS*).
BLACK SWIFT   Uncommon spring migrant and summer visitor, especially when the Cascade foothills are cloaked in clouds (*CSi*).
VAUX'S SWIFT   Common summer visitor.
ANNA'S HUMMINGBIRD   None noted prior to the early 1980s (*ER, KA*). Now common resident and breeder.
RUFOUS HUMMINGBIRD   Reported in summers in 1940s (*HL*). Rare visitor (*ER*) prior to the explosive growth of Himalayan Blackberry in the 1990s. Uncommon summer resident and breeder in the 1990s. Now much scarcer visitor and sometime breeder.
BELTED KINGFISHER   Common visitor, formerly resident.
LEWIS'S WOODPECKER   Rare visitor. One September 3 to 10, 1984 (*ER*). One flying over August 25, 1987; one September 1, 1989 (*KA*).
RED-BREASTED SAPSUCKER   Rare visitor. One early November 1982 (*ER*). One September 17, 1987 (*KA*). One December 5 and 9, 2007 (*BtW*). One March 25, 2009 (*EvH*). One November 11, 2009 (*JeB*). One December 26, 2009 (*CSi*). One January 25, 2010 (*WW*). One March 6, 2010 (*CSi*). One February 3, 2011 (*WW*). One August 30, 2011 (*CSi*). One December 9, 2012 (*RSh*).
DOWNY WOODPECKER   Common resident and breeder.
HAIRY WOODPECKER   Rare visitor. One calling (*HL*). One July 14, 2006 (*GOO*). One January 27, 2013 (*CSi*).
NORTHERN FLICKER   Common resident and breeder. Occasionally, a yellow-shafted appears and contributes to the gene pool.
PILEATED WOODPECKER   Occasional visitor. Most recent sightings: One April 1, 2011 (*EvH*). One May 4, 2011 (*CSi*). One December 11, 2011 (*EC*). One February 3 through March 21, 2012; one May 9 and 17, 2012; a pair May 24, 2012; one October 1, 2012; one December 8, 2012 (*CSi*). One February 27, 2013 (*GOO*). One March 3, 2013; one May 24, 2013 (*CSi*).
OLIVE-SIDED FLYCATCHER   Rare visitor. One May 20, 1981 (*ER*). One August 27, 2003 (*WOS/TAv*.) One August 29, 2008 (*CSi*). One August 10, 2009 (*JeB, CSi*). One August 30, 2010; one May 12, 2011 (*CSi*). One June 6, 2012 (*CSi*).
WESTERN WOOD-PEWEE   Regular migrant. Possible breeder, 2010, 2011 (*CSi*).
WILLOW FLYCATCHER   Common summer breeder in 1940s (*HL*). Now usually a visitor, most common in fall migration. However, singing males present in summer 2009, 2010, 2011 (*CSi, EvH*).
ALDER FLYCATCHER   Rare visitor. One June 12, 2013 (*CSi*).
LEAST FLYCATCHER   Rare visitor. One August 17, 1998 (*WOS/KA*).

DUSKY FLYCATCHER   Rare visitor. One May 17, 2011 (*CSi*).

HAMMOND'S FLYCATCHER   Uncommon migrant; usually one present each spring. Most recent sightings: One April 21, 2012 (*CSi*.) One April 21, 2013 (*EvH, CSi*). One May 8, 2013 (*CSi*).

GRAY FLYCATCHER   Rare visitor. One August 27, 2004 (*WOS/SMa*).

PACIFIC-SLOPE FLYCATCHER   Uncommon migrant.

EASTERN PHOEBE   Rare visitor. One December 8, 2012 (*CSi, JPs*).

SAY'S PHOEBE   Uncommon early spring or fall migrant; usually one present briefly each year. Most recent sighting: March 17 to 23, 2013 (*AlG, CSi, and many observers*).

ASH-THROATED FLYCATCHER   Rare visitor. One August 31, 1975 (*EH*). One August 31, 2009 (*CSi, KL*).

TROPICAL KINGBIRD   Rare visitor. One October 27, 2007 (*WOS/EH*).

WESTERN KINGBIRD   Uncommon spring or fall visitor. Most recent sightings: One May 9, 2011 (*JW*). One May 29, 2011 (*AK*). One April 29, 2012; three June 14 and one June 15, 2012; one July 29, 2012 (*CSi*). One May 1, 2013 (*DPa*).

EASTERN KINGBIRD   One June 17 and 25, 1982; one July 6, 1982 (*ER*). One June 12, 1994 (*CPe*). One June 15, 1996 (*WOS/RR*). One August 9, 1997 (*WOS/TAv*). One June 7, 1998 (*WOS/BB*). One July 18, 1999 (*WOS/TAv*). One August 1, 1999 (*WOS/ST*). One May 29, 2005 (*WOS/TAv*.) One June 10, 2005 (*WOS/LrB*). Two June 19, 2005 (*WOS/DoM*). One May 29, 2006 (*CSi, MtB*). One June 12, 2011 (*CSi*). One June 11, 2012 (*GP*).

SCISSOR-TAILED FLYCATCHER   Rare visitor. One August 2, 2003 (*WOS/SMa, CrM*).

LOGGERHEAD SHRIKE   Rare visitor. One May 25, 1975 (*DP*). One April 10, 1989 (*KA*). One March 31, 2004 (*WOS/DMv*). One April 12, 2008; one March 4 and 5, 2009; one April 5, 2011 (*CSi*).

NORTHERN SHRIKE   Occurred regularly in October in the 1970s and 1980s (*KA*). Now uncommon fall visitor; usually one present each year. Most recent sightings: One October 17, 2011 (*CSi*). One April 13, 2012 (*DPa, GTh*). One juvenile October 14 through November 17, 2012 (*RSp, ASi, CSi, DPa, KAS*). One January 1 through February 17, 2013 (*KP, CSi, DA*).

CASSIN'S VIREO   Rare migrant. One May 1, 1981 (*ER*). One June 18, 1987 (*KA*). Flock on September 3, 2003; one September 5, 2004; one September 3, 2008; one May 23, 2009; one September 10, 2010; one May 12, 2011 (*CSi*).

BLUE-HEADED VIREO   Rare migrant. One September 8, 1995 (*WOS/KA*).

HUTTON'S VIREO   Rare visitor. One April 15 and 19, 2007 (*BtW*). One October 28, 2008 (*KL*). One May 1, 2011 (*IU*). One September 20, 2011 (*CSi*). One October 19, 2012 (*KaS*).

WARBLING VIREO   Regular migrant in spring and fall in small numbers.

RED-EYED VIREO   Rare migrant. Four August 19, 1995 (*WOS/RR*). Two August 24, 1995 (*WOS/DB*). One August 22 and 29, 1996 (*WOS/KA*). One May 17, 2008; one September 2, 2009 (*CSi*). One September 9, 2010; three September 10, 2010 (*KAS*). One May 10, 2013 (*KP*).

STELLER'S JAY   Common resident and breeder, reliably found in Yesler Swamp.

WESTERN SCRUB-JAY   Rare visitor. One September 24, 1998 (*WOS/TAv*). One October 8, 2005 (*Tw/JBr*). One September 26, 2008, observed for a few days (*CSi*). One September 21, 2009, staying through the winter (*KnG, CSi*). One October 1, 2010; joined by as many as six until May 6, 2011 (*CSi, and many observers*). One September 24, 2011; one September 29, 2012 (*CSi*).

BLACK-BILLED MAGPIE   Rare visitor. One March 9, 2013 (*TC, CSi*).

AMERICAN CROW   Common resident. Nested near kiosk, spring 2011; nested in Yesler Swamp, spring 2013 (*CSi*).

COMMON RAVEN   Rare visitor. One March 11, 2009; one March 11, 2013 (*CSi*).

Chipping Sparrow near Douglas Road © Joe Sweeney

HORNED LARK Scarce migrant (usually very late fall), seen one or two dates each year up to 2000s. Now rare. Most recent sightings: One December 4 and 5, 2005 (*MtB*; *WOS/TAv*, *JB*, *MiH*). One September 12, 2009 (*CSi*, *TK*).

PURPLE MARTIN Common summer visitor and fall migrant in the 1940s (*HL*) up to the 1970s (*KA*). Now occasional migrant. Most recently sightings: More than thirty August 16, 2011; more than fifty September 20, 2011; two August 15, 2012 (*CSi*).

TREE SWALLOW Common summer resident and breeder.

VIOLET-GREEN SWALLOW Common summer resident and breeder.

NORTHERN ROUGH-WINGED SWALLOW Uncommon migrant; a few seen every year.

BANK SWALLOW Rare migrant. One May 30 through June 4, 1980; one September 4, 1980; one April 24, 1981 (*ER*). One August 21 and September 1, 1993 (*WOS/RTh*). One May 12, 1998 (*WOS/BB*). One August 9, 2003 (*WOS/SMa*). One May 11, 2004 (*WOS/SMa*). One August 27, 2004; one March 19, 2008; three August 3, 2010; three May 22, 2012; one September 5, 2012; three May 19, 2013 (*CSi*).

CLIFF SWALLOW Common summer resident and breeder.

BARN SWALLOW Common summer resident and breeder; occasionally present in other seasons, though not as year-round resident.

BLACK-CAPPED CHICKADEE Common resident and breeder.

CHESTNUT-BACKED CHICKADEE Uncommon visitor. Most recent sightings: One March 6, 2009; one October 6, 2010 (*EvH*). One February 21, 2011 (*SR*). Two July 9, 2011 (*EvH*). One August 9, 2012 (*CSi*).

BUSHTIT Common resident and breeder.

RED-BREASTED NUTHATCH Uncommon visitor, becoming more regular as tree cover increases.

BROWN CREEPER   Uncommon resident and breeder.
BEWICK'S WREN   Common resident and breeder.
HOUSE WREN   Rare visitor. One August 7, 2004; one August 18, 2007; one May 9, 2009; one August 25, 2010; one April 20, 2012; one June 4, 2013 (*CSi*).
PACIFIC WREN   Uncommon winter resident; most often found in Yesler Swamp and along the treeline in Sidles Swamp.
MARSH WREN   Common resident and breeder.
GOLDEN-CROWNED KINGLET   Common visitor, most often seen in winter and during migration.
RUBY-CROWNED KINGLET   Common winter resident.
TOWNSEND'S SOLITAIRE   Rare visitor. One May 5, 2012 (*JEl*).
MOUNTAIN BLUEBIRD   Rare visitor. One October 18,1984 (*ER*). One May 14, 1994 (*WOS/TP*). One September 28, 2007 (*WOS/MkW*). Two females April 3, 2009 (*CSi*). One female April 12, 2010 (*CSi*).
SWAINSON'S THRUSH   Uncommon summer resident in the 1940s (*HL*). Recorded most years in the 1970s and 1980s (*KA*). Now uncommon migrant. Most recent sightings: One April 7, 2009 (*CSi, EvH*). Two April 25, 2009 (*KAS*). One May 15, 2010 (*CSi*). One September 2, 2010 (*EvH*). One May 22, 2011; one August 31, 2011; one May 17, 2012; one May 2, 2013 (*CSi*).
HERMIT THRUSH   Uncommon migrant and winter resident. Most recent sightings: Two April 24, 2009 (*CSi*). Two April 25, 2009 (*CSi, KAS*). One October 22, 2009; one December 7, 2009; one April 26, 2010 (*CSi*). One November 24, 2010 (*EvH*). One April 21, 2011; one January 1, 2013 (*CSi*). Two April 21, 2013 (*EvH*).
AMERICAN ROBIN   Common resident and breeder.
VARIED THRUSH   Uncommon visitor; usually at least one present in winter, spring, or fall.
NORTHERN MOCKINGBIRD   Rare visitor. One October 28, 1993 (*WOS/KA, DB*).
BROWN THRASHER   Rare visitor. One June 12, 2011 (*CSi*).
SAGE THRASHER   Rare visitor. One May 11 through 24, 2002 (*WOS/DP, CSi*).
EUROPEAN STARLING   Common resident and breeder.
AMERICAN PIPIT   Uncommon visitor. Most common in September, October, April, and May; sometimes overwinters. High count: More than sixty on September 16, 2006 (*CSi*).
CEDAR WAXWING   Common though sporadic; nested in 2008 (*CSi*).
TENNESSEE WARBLER   Rare migrant. One September 8, 1995 (*WOS/KA*) and again September 9 (*WOS/GT*). One August 19, 2009 (*CSi*).
ORANGE-CROWNED WARBLER   Common migrant.
NASHVILLE WARBLER   Rare migrant. One September 10, 1985 (*KA*). One September 25, 1994 (*WOS/DMc*). One September 10, 2005 (*WOS/TKL*). One September 30, 2005 (*WOS/KA*). One April 28, 2007; one April 26, 2008 (*CSi*). One May 10, 2008 (*EvH*). One May 12, 2008; one August 22, 2008 (*MtB*). One April 24, 2009 (*CSi*). One May 9, 2009 (*Seattle Audubon Board Birdathon*). One May 12, 2011 (*PK*). One September 5, 2011 (*TN*). One May 9, 2012 (*CSi*).
YELLOW WARBLER   Common migrant and occasional breeder.
YELLOW-RUMPED WARBLER   Common migrant and winter resident. Both forms, Myrtle and Audubon's, are present.
BLACK-THROATED GRAY WARBLER   Uncommon migrant. Usually at least one or two found each spring and fall. Unusually high numbers of individuals mid-August 2009 (*JeB, EvH, CSi*).
TOWNSEND'S WARBLER   Occasional winter visitor or migrant; usually at least one present each year. Most recent sightings: One May 22, 2011 (*CSi*). One April 21, 2012 (*AL*). One April 26, 2013 (*CSi*).

Palm Warbler   Rare visitor. One September 13 to 17, 1993 (*WOS/EN*). One September 20, 1998 (*WOS/BB*). One December 30, 2000 through April 15, 2001 (*WOS/RL and many observers*).
American Redstart   Rare migrant. One August 26 to 28, 1988 (*KA, TH, BSu*). One August 19 to September 3, 1990 (*KA, HO, EH*). One September 4, 2000 (*MB*).
Northern Waterthrush   Rare migrant. One August 17, 1989 (*KA*). One August 30, 1998 (*WOS/BV*). One August 21, 2003 (*WOS/TAv*).
MacGillivray's Warbler   Rare migrant. One September 21, 1980; one April 30, 1981; one May 3, 1981; one May 18, 1982 (*ER*). One September 10, 1985; one August 16, 1989; one August 24, 1989 (*KA*). One August 24, 1995 (*WOS/DB*). One August 18, 1998 (*WOS/TAv*). One September 1998 (*BV*). One August 15, 2004 (*WOS/TAv*). One May 21 and 30, 2008; one June 4, 2008; one August 12, 2008 (*MtB*). One August 19, 2009 (*CSi, JeB*). One August 15, 2010; one August 10, 2011 (*CSi*). One May 20, 2012 (*EvH*.)
Common Yellowthroat   Common summer resident and breeder.
Wilson's Warbler   Common migrant.
Western Tanager   Uncommon spring and fall migrant.
Spotted Towhee   Common resident and breeder.
American Tree Sparrow   Rare winter visitor. One January 11 and 15, 1981; one October 15 and November 7, 1981 (*ER*). One October 21, 1993 (*WOS/RTh*). One October 24, 2008; one February 21, 2009 (*CSi*). Formerly more common, averaging one or two a year (*KA*).
Chipping Sparrow   Occasional visitor. Most recent sightings: One April 7, 2009 (*EvH*). One April 14, 2009; one June 5, 2011 (*CSi*). One June 1, 2013 (*JS*).
Clay-colored Sparrow   Rare visitor. One November 7, 1999 (*CSi*). One April 28, 2008 (*MtB*). One September 5 and 6, 2008 (*WOS/JeB; CSi*).
Brewer's Sparrow   Rare visitor. One April 27, 1995 (*WOS/CH*). One September 22, 1998 (*WOS/TAv*).
Vesper Sparrow   Rare visitor. One April 18, 1973 (*FK*). One May 8, 1976 (*KA*). One September 23 and 29, 1981 (*ER*). One September 5 to 12, 1985; one September 11, 1986 (*KA*). One April 29, 1996 (*WOS/MS*). One April 21, 1998 (*WOS/BB*). One September 24, 2002 (*WOS/MiH*). One September 1 to 10, 2005 (*WOS/KA, TKL*). One September 9, 2008; one April 5, 2009 (*CSi*). One September 2, 2010 (*RL*). One September 12, 2010 (*CSi*).
Lark Sparrow   Rare visitor. One May 14, 1993 (*THa*). One August 12, 2007 (*CSi*).
Black-throated Sparrow   Rare visitor. One May 19, 1989 (*KA*).
Sage Sparrow   Rare visitor. One February 17 to 19, 1980 (*EH*). One March 14 to 15, 1987, 1987 (*DBe*).
Savannah Sparrow   Common summer resident and breeder.
Fox Sparrow   Fairly common winter resident.
Song Sparrow   Common resident and breeder.
Lincoln's Sparrow   Common winter resident.
Swamp Sparrow   Rare visitor. One November 20, 1987 (*KA*). One seen frequently from November 20 through December 24, 1995 (*WOS/DMc*). One April 14, 1996 (*WOS/DMc*). One April 5, 2005 (*WOS/ST, DnF*). One seen frequently in April 2008 (*CSi*). One January 10, 2013 (*WW*). One February 23 through 26, 2013 (*CSi*).
White-throated Sparrow   Rare visitor. One October 4, 1981 (*ER*). One October 26, 1984 (*KA*). One October 7, 1993 (*WOS/RR*). One September 30, 1998 (*WOS/Tw*). One October 26, 2003 (*CSi*). One March 19, 2007 (*MtB*). One April 18 and 19, 2009 (*CSi*). One January 3 and 7, 2010 (*VJK; EvH; CSi*). One January 25, 2011 (*CSi*).
Harris's Sparrow   Rare visitor. One November 10, 1974 (*FK*). One November 1992 (*CSi*). One November 23 through December 18, 1993 (*WOS/LCo, RTh, DMc*).
White-crowned Sparrow   Common resident and summer breeder (*pugetensis* subspecies more common; *gambelli* seen mostly in migration).

GOLDEN-CROWNED SPARROW   Common winter resident.
DARK-EYED JUNCO   Common winter resident, reliably found in Yesler Swamp.
CHESTNUT-COLLARED LONGSPUR   Rare migrant. One December 3 through 12, 1995 (*MS*, *CSi*, *WOS/CM*).
MCCOWN'S LONGSPUR   Rare migrant. One June 8, 2013 (*HG*, *HN*, *MW*).
LAPLAND LONGSPUR   Regular fall migrant in 1980s (*KA*). Most recent sighting: October 6 through 18, 2007 (*WOS/BtW*, *MiH*, *MtB*, *CSi*).
SNOW BUNTING   Rare visitor. One November 1975; one February 1976 (*KA*).
ROSE-BREASTED GROSBEAK   Rare visitor. One June 1 and 3, 2003 (*WOS/RSh*, *MiD*).
BLACK-HEADED GROSBEAK   Uncommon migrant and sometime summer visitor.
LAZULI BUNTING   Rare visitor and breeder (evidence of breeding in 2008). One May 25, 1974 (*FK*). One June 29 and July 9, 1983 (*ER*). One August 19, 1988 (*KA*). One July 22, 1998 (*WOS/TAv*). One May 10, 2004 (*WOS/SMa*). One pair and possibly one other male, summer 2008; male first recorded June 1; immature recorded that year (*CSi*, *EvH*). Two males May 10, 2009 (*EvH*). A pair June 17, 2009 (*JeB*). One May 29, 2010 (*CSi*). Three June 7, 2010 (*EvH*). Two June 15 and one June 20, 2012; one May 17 through June 2, 2013; four (three males and one female) May 30, 2013 (*CSi*).
INDIGO BUNTING   Rare visitor. One September 14, 1988 (*KA*). One June 1, 1996 (*WOS*).
BOBOLINK   Rare visitor. One May 25, 1979; one June 2 and 3, 1980; one May 28, 1981; one September 3 and 14, 1981 (*EH*). One August 15, 1982; one October 10, 1983 (*ER*). One October 1 and 2, 1995 (*DP*; *WOS/BSu*).
RED-WINGED BLACKBIRD   Common summer resident and breeder; also common as migrant.
WESTERN MEADOWLARK   Former common summer resident in the 1940s (*HL*), now regular visitor in spring and fall. Three overwintered in 2008 (*CSi*) and one in 2009 (*CSi*).
YELLOW-HEADED BLACKBIRD   Uncommon migrant. Most recent sightings: May 7, 2010; May 4, 2011 (*CSi*). One June 11, 2011 (*TK*). A pair May 11, 2012; one August 25, 2012; one seen off and on from May 4 through June 1, 2013 (*CSi*, *JS*).
RUSTY BLACKBIRD   Rare visitor. One October 5 through 8, 1993 (*WOS/EN*, *KA*). One September 24, 1994 (*WOS/EN*). One October 31 to November 5, 1995 (*WOS/KA*, *EN*).
BREWER'S BLACKBIRD   Common summer resident and breeder, with a colony in the bushes around the helipad.
BROWN-HEADED COWBIRD   Common summer resident and breeder.
BULLOCK'S ORIOLE   Uncommon summer visitor and occasional summer resident. One pair nested in 1986. Most recent sightings: One May 1, 2008 (*MtB*). One June 4, 2009 (*EvH*). One May 28, 2011 (*EvH*). One June 30, 2011 (*JZ*).
GRAY-CROWNED ROSY-FINCH   Rare visitor. Nine November 30, 1973 (*FK*).
PURPLE FINCH   Occasional visitor, most often in migration but sometimes in other seasons. Reported breeding, spring 2009 (*JeB*).
HOUSE FINCH   Common resident and breeder.
RED CROSSBILL   Rare visitor, usually flyover. One flock of fifteen May 2, 1985. Flock of eight, April 19, 2009 (*JeB*); five seen on same day (*KAS*, *HG*, *HN*). Large flock April 22, 2009 (*EvH*, *CSi*). Two January 2, 2013 (*AlG*). Seventeen January 6, 2013; then numerous sightings of from two to fifty-plus through June 2, 2013 (*CSi*, *GOO*).
COMMON REDPOLL   Rare winter visitor. A flock of twenty-eight on February 3, 1982 (*ER*). One January 8, 2012 (*GOO*).
PINE SISKIN   Common visitor in spring, fall, and winter; can be present in large flocks.
AMERICAN GOLDFINCH   Common resident, less common as a breeder.
EVENING GROSBEAK   Uncommon visitor, usually flyover. Most recent sightings: One May 23, 2009 (*CSi*). One October 17 and 31, 2010 (*EvH*). One September 30, 2011; two August 26, 2012 (*CSi*).

HOUSE SPARROW Uncommon resident and breeder; more common in surrounding neighborhood.

Observers
(listed alphabetically by last name)

KA Kevin Aanerud (note: most observations are from "Birds Observed at Montlake Fill, University of Washington Campus, Seattle, Washington, from 1972 to 1989" in *Washington Birds* 1 (December 1989): 6-21; some observations are reports Kevin made to WOS since that date and are documented in WOS records); *DA* Darwin Alonso; *JA* Janine Anderson; *KAn* Kathy Andrich; *TAv* Tom Aversa

JBr Jessie Barry; *MtB* Matt Bartels; *KB* K. Barton; *BlB* Blair Bernson; *DBe* Dave Beaudette; *FB* Fred Bird; *BB* BirdBox (telephone hotline, published in *WOSNews)*; *TB* Thais Bock; *LrB* Lauren Braden; *JB* Jan Bragg; *MB* Marc Breuninger; *JeB* Jeffrey Bryant; *DB* David Buckley

PCa Pam Cahn; *PCr* Peter Carr; *EC* Else Cobb; *TC* Tom Cogbill; *LCo* Luke Cole; *CCx* Cameron Cox; *PC* Paul Cozens

AmD Amy Davis; *ED* Ed Deal; *EDo* Ed Dominguez; *MiD* Michael Dossett; *RD* Rick Droker; *MtD* Matt Dufort; *PDu* Peter Dunwiddie

MEg Mark Egger; *JEl* Jim Elder

JiF Jim Flynn; *DnF* Dan Froehlich

HG Helen Gilbert; *KnG* Ken Grant; *AlG* Alan Grenon

TH Todd Haas; *THa* T. Hahn; *PHa* Pete Hammill; *JHe* John Hebert; *DH* David Hepp; *HL* Harry W. Higman and Earl J. Larrison from their book, *Union Bay: The Life of a City Marsh* (University of Washington Press: 1951); *CH* Chris Hill; *MiH* Michael Hobbs; *MaH* Marc Hoffman; *EvH* Evan Houston; *EH* Eugene (Gene) Hunn

VJK Vicki and Jim King; *LKi* Lann Kittleson; *TKL* Tina Klein-Lebbink; *AK* A. Kopitov; *PK* Penny Koyama; *FK* Fayette F. Krause (from *Birds of the University of Washington Campus* (Seattle: Thomas Burke Memorial Washington State Museum, University of Washington, 1975); *TK* Tim Kuhn

AL Abby Larson; *NLr* Norma Larson; *RL* Rachel Lawson; *TL* Terry LeLievre; *KL* Kathrine Lloyd

DMc Dan MacDougall-Treacy; *SMa* Stuart MacKay; *AM* Alexandra MacKenzie; *TM* Tom Mansfield; *DoM* Douglas Marshal; *MFM* MaryFrances Mathis; *BMc* Brendan McGarry; *CM* Chris McInerny (note: most observations are from "Shorebird Passage at the Montlake Fill, University of Washington, Seattle, 1996-1997," in *Washington Birds* 8 (November 2002):19-28. Some observations are reports Chris made to WOS and are documented in WOS records); *DMv* Don McVay; *RyM* Ryan Merrill; *MM* Mary Metz; *CrM* Craig Miller; *MC* Robert C. Miller and Elizabeth L. Curtis, "Birds of the University of Washington Campus," in *The Murrelet* 21:2, pp. 35-46 (May-August 1940); *KM* Kathryn Murphy

TN Terry Nightingale; *HN* Henry Noble; *EN* Erica Norwood

GOO Grace and Ollie Oliver; *HO* Hal Opperman

GP George Pagos; *DPa* Doug Parrott; *DP* Dennis Paulson; *CPe* Curtis Pearson; *TP* Ted Peterson; ***KP*** Kevin Purcell; ***JPs*** John Puschock

SR Scott Ramos; ***ER*** Ellen S. Ratoosh (from "Birds of the Montlake Fill, Seattle, Washington (1979-1983)," in *Washington Birds* 4 (December 1995): 1-34); ***RR*** Russell Rogers; ***FR*** Fred Rowley; ***EmR*** Emily Runnells

MSc Michael Schrimpf; ***DSu*** Doug Schurman; ***AdS*** Adam Sedgley; ***RSh*** Ryan Shaw; ***ASi*** Alex Sidles; ***CSi*** Constance Sidles; ***JAS*** John Sidles; ***KaS*** Kathy Slettebak; ***KAS*** Kathy and Arn Slettebak; ***MS*** Mike Smith; ***RSp*** Rachel Sprague; ***RSt*** Rose Stogsdill; ***BSu*** Bob Sundstrom; ***JS*** Joe Sweeney

ST Sam Terry; ***GTh*** Gregg Thompson; ***RTh*** Rob Thorn; ***GT*** Greg Toffic; ***JTb*** John Tubbs; ***Tw*** Tweeters

IU Idie Ulsh

BV Bob Vandenbosch; ***MVe*** Mark Vernon

WOS Washington Ornithological Society (in "Washington Field Notes," published in *WOS-News* each issue); ***MkW*** Mike West; ***WW*** Woody Wheeler; ***MW*** Mike Wile; ***JW*** Jacqueline Williams; ***BtW*** Brett Wolfe

RY Richard Youel

JZ Jim Zook

Great Blue Heron © Doug Parrott

Index

Adams, Ansel, 70
Affleck, Ben, 59
Alabaster, 35–38
Alder Flycatcher, *see* Flycatcher, Alder
Amadeus, 53
American Avocet, *see* Avocet, American
American Beaver, *see* Beaver, American
American Bittern, *see* Bittern, American
American Black Duck, *see* Duck, American Black
American Coot, *see* Coot, American
American Crow, *see* Crow, American
American Golden-Plover, *see* Plover, American Golden-
American Goldfinch, *see* Goldfinch, American
American Kestrel, *see* Kestrel, American
American Pipit, *see* Pipit, American
American Redstart, *see* Redstart, American
American Robin, *see* Robin, American
American Tree Sparrow, *see* Sparrow, American Tree
American White Pelican, *see* Pelican, American White
American Wigeon, *see* Wigeon, American
Ammirati, Joe, 189
And Live Rejoicing, 192
Anna's Hummingbird, *see* Hummingbird, Anna's
Aristotle, 148
Ash-throated Flycatcher, *see* Flycatcher, Ash-throated
Aunt Marie
    airplane worries, 71–73
    care of material things, 20
    faith in tough times, 165–168
    learning new things, 174
    temperament, 71
Averroes, 89–91
Avocet, American, 226

Baird's Sandpiper, *see* Sandpiper, Baird's

Bald Eagle, *see* Eagle, Bald
Band-tailed Pigeon, *see* Pigeon, Band-tailed
Bank Swallow, *see* Swallow, Bank
Barn Owl, *see* Owl, Barn
Barn Swallow, *see* Swallow, Barn
Barred Owl, *see* Owl, Barred
Barrow's Goldeneye, *see* Goldeneye, Barrow's
Baseball diamond, 63, 66, 93, 140
Beaver, American
    photograph, **33**
Belted Kingfisher, *see* Kingfisher, Belted
Ben Hur, 177
Bent Pyramid, 82
Bewick's Wren, *see* Wren, Bewick's
Bieber, Justin, 30
Bird brain, 144
    American Coot, 196
    anatomy, 25
    Black-capped Chickadee, 23
    Pine Siskin, 39
"Bird Stone", **220**
Birdsall, Mel, 193
Bittern, American, 224
Black Swift, *see* Swift, Black
Black Tern, *see* Tern, Black
Black-bellied Plover, *see* Plover, Black-bellied
Black-billed Magpie, *see* Magpie, Black-billed
Black-capped Chickadee, *see* Chickadee, Black-capped
Black-crowned Night-Heron, *see* Heron, Black-crowned Night-
Black-headed Grosbeak, *see* Grosbeak, Black-headed
Black-headed Gull, *see* Gull, Black-headed
Black-necked Stilt, *see* Stilt, Black-necked
Black-throated Gray Warbler, *see* Warbler, Black-throated Gray

Black-throated Sparrow, *see* Sparrow,
    Black-throated
Blackbird
    Brewer's, 80, 86, 234
        photograph, **83**
    Red-winged, 58, 188, 234
        photograph, **187**
    Rusty, 234
    Yellow-headed, 234
Blue Forest, North, 45
Blue Forest, South, 59
Blue-headed Vireo, *see* Vireo,
    Blue-headed
Blue-winged Teal, *see* Teal, Blue-winged
Bluebird, Mountain, 232
Bobolink, 234
Bobwhite, Northern, 224
Bonaparte's Gull, *see* Gull, Bonaparte's
Borges, Jorge Luis, 89–91
Bowen, Barbara A., **206**
Boy Scout Pond, 39
Brant, 221
Brems, James, **220**
Brewer's Blackbird, *see* Blackbird,
    Brewer's
Brewer's Sparrow, *see* Sparrow, Brewer's
Brown Creeper, *see* Creeper, Brown
Brown Thrasher, *see* Thrasher, Brown
Brown-headed Cowbird, *see* Cowbird,
    Brown-headed
Buff-breasted Sandpiper, *see* Sandpiper,
    Buff-breasted
Bufflehead, **214**, 223
Bug Look, 32, 141
Bullfrog
    photograph, **57**
Bullock's Oriole, *see* Oriole, Bullock's
Bunting
    Indigo, 234
    Lazuli, 234
    Snow, 234
Burns, George, 61
Bushtit, 23, 231
    photograph, **25**
Butterfly
    Milbert's Tortoiseshell
        photograph, **23**
    Mourning Cloak, 44
        photograph, **43**

Cackling Goose, *see* Goose, Cackling
California Gull, *see* Gull, California
California Quail, *see* Quail, California
Campbell, Joseph, 50
Canada Goose, *see* Goose, Canada
Canal Road, 93, 140
Canoe Island, 53
Canvasback, 223
    photograph, **222**
Caroline Kline Galland Home, 111
Caspian Tern, *see* Tern, Caspian
Cassin's Vireo, *see* Vireo, Cassin's
Cattle Egret, *see* Egret, Cattle
Cedar Waxwing, *see* Waxwing, Cedar
Chestnut-backed Chickadee, *see*
    Chickadee, Chestnut-backed
Chestnut-collared Longspur, *see*
    Longspur, Chestnut-collared
Chickadee
    Black-capped, 21–24, 231
        photograph, **22**
    Chestnut-backed, 231
Chipping Sparrow, *see* Sparrow,
    Chipping
*Christopher Columbus and the Conquest of
    Paradise*, 122
Cinnabar Moth, *see* Moth, Cinnabar
Cinnamon Teal, *see* Teal, Cinnamon
Clark's Grebe, *see* Grebe, Clark's
Clay-colored Sparrow, *see* Sparrow,
    Clay-colored
Cliff Swallow, *see* Swallow, Cliff
Colm, Fergie, 59
Common Goldeneye, *see* Goldeneye,
    Common
Common Loon, *see* Loon, Common
Common Merganser, *see* Merganser,
    Common
Common Nighthawk, *see* Nighthawk,
    Common
Common Poorwill, *see* Poorwill,
    Common
Common Raven, *see* Raven, Common
Common Redpoll, *see* Redpoll, Common
Common Teal, *see* Teal, Eurasian
Common Tern, *see* Tern, Common
Common Yellowthroat, *see* Yellowthroat,
    Common
Conibear, 9

Index

Cooper's Hawk, *see* Hawk, Cooper's
Coot, American, 180, 195–196, 225
    photograph, **198**
Cormorant, Double-crested, 63–67, 224
    photograph, **64, 65**
Corporation Yard Pond, 45
Cosby, Bill, 62
Cowbird, Brown-headed, 234
Cowell, Simon, 16
Coyote, 45, 176
    photograph, **50**
Crane, Sandhill, 226
Creeper, Brown, 232
Crossbill, Red, 234
Crow, American, 230

Dark-eyed Junco, *see* Junco, Dark-eyed
The Day the Earth Stood Still, 148
Dempsey Gym, 52
Djoser, King, 81
Double-crested Cormorant, *see*
    Cormorant, Double-crested
Dove
    Eurasian Collared-, 192, 228
    Mourning, 228
Dowitcher
    Long-billed, 154, 228
        photograph, **155**
    Short-billed, 228
Downy Woodpecker, *see* Woodpecker,
    Downy
Doyle, Jim, 40
Dragonfly painting, **213**
Drumheller Fountain, 52
Duck
    American Black, 223
    Long-tailed, 223
    Ring-necked, 223
    Ruddy, 224
    Tufted, 27–31, 223
        photograph, **28**
    Wood, 73, 74, **211**, 223
Dunlin, 226
    photograph, **227**
Dusky Flycatcher, *see* Flycatcher, Dusky
Duvall, Robert, 169

Eagle
    Bald, 105, 180, 195, **215**, 225
    Golden, 225
Eared Grebe, *see* Grebe, Eared
East Point, 13, 27, 29, 34, 103, 195
Eastern Kingbird, *see* Kingbird, Eastern
Eastern Phoebe, *see* Phoebe, Eastern
Ecological balance, 84
Eeyore, 192
Egret
    Cattle, 225
    Great, 225
Eliphaz, 192
Emperor Goose, *see* Goose, Emperor
Eurasian Collared-Dove, *see* Dove,
    Eurasian Collared-
Eurasian Teal, *see* Teal, Eurasian
Eurasian Wigeon, *see* Wigeon, Eurasian
European Starling, *see* Starling, European
Evening Grosbeak, *see* Grosbeak,
    Evening

Fabio, 30
Fairy tale
    Black Swifts, 128
    falcon and panther, 6–7
    money, 152
Falcon, Peregrine, 88, 225
Feathers, 53
Fiddler on the Roof, 193
Finch
    Gray-crowned Rosy-, 234
    House, 234
    Purple, 234
Flicker, Northern, 116–118, 122, 229
    photograph, **117**
"Flight"
    photograph, **206**
Flycatcher
    Alder, 229
    Ash-throated, 230
    Dusky, 230
    Gray, 230
    Hammond's, 230
    Least, 229
    Olive-sided, 229
    Pacific-slope, 230
    Scissor-tailed, 230
    Willow, 229
Fox Sparrow, *see* Sparrow, Fox
Franklin's Gull, *see* Gull, Franklin's

Friends of Yesler Swamp, 189

Gable, Clark, 34
Gadwall, 223
Garden
    Center for Urban Horticulture
        photograph, **51**
Glaucous-winged Gull, *see* Gull,
    Glaucous-winged
Gold's Gym, 3
Golden Eagle, *see* Eagle, Golden
Golden-crowned Kinglet, *see* Kinglet,
    Golden-crowned
Golden-crowned Sparrow, *see* Sparrow,
    Golden-crowned
Goldeneye
    Barrow's, 224
    Common, 224
Goldfinch, American, 93–95, 159, 234
    photograph, **96**
Goose
    Cackling, 221
    Canada, 221
    Emperor, 221
    Greater White-fronted, 221
    Ross's, 221
    Snow, 221
Gort, 148
Goshawk, Northern, 225
Gray Flycatcher, *see* Flycatcher, Gray
Gray-crowned Rosy-Finch, *see* Finch,
    Gray-crowned Rosy-
Great Blue Heron, *see* Heron, Great Blue
Great Egret, *see* Egret, Great
Great Horned Owl, *see* Owl, Great
    Horned
Greater Scaup, *see* Scaup, Greater
Greater White-fronted Goose, *see* Goose,
    Greater White-fronted
Greater Yellowlegs, *see* Yellowlegs,
    Greater
Grebe
    Clark's, 224
    Eared, 224
    Horned, 224
    Pied-billed, 110, 224
        photograph, **iv**, **112**
    Red-necked, 224
    Western, 176–178, 224
        photograph, **179**
Green Heron, *see* Heron, Green
Green-winged Teal, *see* Teal,
    Green-winged
Gregoire, Christine, 40
Grosbeak
    Black-headed, 234
    Evening, 234
    Rose-breasted, 234
Gull
    Black-headed, 228
    Bonaparte's, 228
    California, 228
    Franklin's, 228
    Glaucous-winged, 228
    Herring, 228
    Mew, 228
    Ring-billed, 228
    Sabine's, 125
    Thayer's, 228
    Western, 228

Hairy Woodpecker, *see* Woodpecker,
    Hairy
Hamilton, Ethel, **206**
Hammond's Flycatcher, *see* Flycatcher,
    Hammond's
Harrier, Northern, 225
Harris's Sparrow, *see* Sparrow, Harris's
Harryman, Doug, 200
Hashimoto, Molly, **211**
Hawk
    Cooper's, 2, 39, 88, 159–160, 225
        photograph, **42**, **79**
    Red-shouldered, 225
    Red-tailed, 88, 184, 225
    Rough-legged, 225
    Sharp-shinned, 88, 225
Hawking, Stephen, 70
Heitzman, LuElla, **206**
Helipad, 80
Helmsley, Leona, 197
Hermit Thrush, *see* Thrush, Hermit
Heron
    Black-crowned Night-, 225
    Great Blue, 52–56, 73, 103, 205, 224
        photograph, **54**, **55**, **236**
        rookery, 53
    Green, 159, 225

photograph, **201**
Herring Gull, *see* Gull, Herring
Hitchens, Pat, 125, 126
Hokusai, 48
Honda Insight, 148
Hooded Merganser, *see* Merganser, Hooded
Horned Grebe, *see* Grebe, Horned
Horned Lark, *see* Lark, Horned
House Finch, *see* Finch, House
House Sparrow, *see* Sparrow, House
House Wren, *see* Wren, House
Houston, Alice, 44
Houston, Evan, **92**
Hummingbird
    Anna's, 59, 192, 229
        photograph, **60**
    Rufous, 192, 229
Hunn Meadow West, 71
Hurley, Matthew, 31
Hutton's Vireo, *see* Vireo, Hutton's
Hydra, 122

Important Bird Area, 66
Indigo Bunting, *see* Bunting, Indigo
Interconnectedness, 41, 84, 99, 146

Japan Encyclopedia, 48
Jay
    Steller's, 230
        Western Scrub-, 230
Job, 192
Johnson, Lewis E., **19**, **33**, **51**, **151**
Joseph II, Emperor, 53
Junco, Dark-eyed, 234

Keillor, Garrison, 25
Kern's Restoration Pond, 141
Kestrel, American, 93–95, 225
    photograph, **97**
Killdeer, 164–165, 226
    photograph, **92**, **167**
King Tut, *see* Tutankhamun, King
King, Martin Luther, Jr., 140
Kingbird
    Eastern, 230
    Tropical, 230
    Western, 230
Kingfisher, Belted, 160, 229

photograph, **162**
Kinglet
    Golden-crowned, 23, 163, 232
    Ruby-crowned, 23, 59, 232
        photograph, **61**
Kuhn, Tim, **iv**, **14**, **18**, **22**, **25**, **37**, **60**, **69**, **79**, **83**, **104**, **133**, **158**, **171**

Lancaster, Burt, 34
Lapland Longspur, *see* Longspur, Lapland
Lark Sparrow, *see* Sparrow, Lark
Lark, Horned, 231
Lazuli Bunting, *see* Bunting, Lazuli
Least Flycatcher, *see* Flycatcher, Least
Least Sandpiper, *see* Sandpiper, Least
Lesser Scaup, *see* Scaup, Lesser
Lesser Yellowlegs, *see* Yellowlegs, Lesser
Lewis's Woodpecker, *see* Woodpecker, Lewis's
Life lessons
    anticipation, 108
    beauty within, 78
    birding with children, 103–106
    bloody-mindedness, 85–86
    bogged down by others' sins, 193
    Bug Look, 32, 141
    building community, 200
    changing the world, 168
    children in our lives, 115
    community, 144–146
    competition, 95–100
    confidence in your beliefs, 169
    consumerism, 156
    creating hope, 140
    defining the good life, 149
    disabled in spirit, 71
    empty nest, 12–13
    engaged in the moment, 161
    expectations, 106–109
    farmwife gone wild, 186
    finding the good in people, 178
    gadgets control you, 20
    getting old, 61–62
    good angels, 200
    graciousness, 178
    helicopter mom, 160
    home, 119–122
    how to be happy, 192

identity, 197
John's trophy, 99
joys of ordinary life, 127
kindness, pass it forward, 199
laughter, 32
learn by doing, 173
little people, 199
love of lists, 48
loved ones live in you, 38
making the best of it, 135–139
money, 152–158
nature of beauty, 57
nests, 118
nuanced beauty, 78
our differences, 44
our values, 84
overcoming prejudice, 44
plumage as signifier, 31
retirement, 184–188
true or untrue beliefs, 169
understanding others, 180
us vs. them, 40
ways to join together, 44
web of life, 111
wonder, 132
world ugly and beautiful, 79
worries, 161
Lincoln's Sparrow, see Sparrow, Lincoln's
Lloyd, Kathrine, 8, **50**, **121**, **167**, **182**, **205**
Loggerhead Shrike, see Shrike, Loggerhead
Lone Pine Tree, 9, 184
Long-billed Dowitcher, see Dowitcher, Long-billed
Long-tailed Duck, see Duck, Long-tailed
Longspur
  Chestnut-collared, 234
  Lapland, 234
  McCown's, 234
Loon
  Common, 224
  Red-throated, 224
Loop Trail, 9, 17, 59, 134, 144, 146, 163, 188

MacGillivray's Warbler, see Warbler, MacGillivray's
MacKenzie, Alexandra, **1**, **210**
Madsen, Ethan, **208**

Magic, 132
Magpie, Black-billed, 230
Main Pond, 2, 74, 94, 126, 147, 150, 154, 159, 184, **209**
Mallard, 58, 123, 126, 223
  photograph, **124**
Marina, 9
Marsh Wren, see Wren, Marsh
Martin, Purple, 231
Matsen, Rick, 200
May Day, 113
McCann, Hub, 169
McCown's Longspur, see Longspur, McCown's
Meadowlark, Western, 71, 234
Merganser
  Common, 34–35, 224
    photograph, **36, 37**
  Hooded, 2, 224
    photograph, **4**
  Red-breasted, 224
Merlin, 88, 165, 225
  photograph, **166**
Merrill, Ryan, **46**
Mew Gull, see Gull, Mew
Milbert's Tortoiseshell butterfly , see Butterfly, Milbert's Tortoiseshell
Mockingbird, Northern, 232
Modoc, 172, 174
Money, 152–158
Monson, Shirley, **206**
Montlake Fill
  as inspiration for art, 204
  fog most magical, 15
  history, 204
  map, 202–203
  nibbled away, 80
  scraggliness, 56–57
  vistas, 45
Moth, Cinnabar
  photograph, **109**
Mounce, Lili, 178
Mountain Bluebird, see Bluebird, Mountain
Mourning Cloak butterfly, see Butterfly, Mourning Cloak
Mourning Dove, see Dove, Mourning
Mozart, Wolfgang, 53
Mr. Rogers, see Rogers, Fred

Mullet, 30
Mushrooms, 189
Muskrat
  photograph, **19**
Mute Swan, *see* Swan, Mute

Nashville Warbler, *see* Warbler, Nashville
Neuman, Alfred E., 2
Nighthawk, Common, 229
Nixon, Richard, 88
North Blue Forest, *see* Blue Forest, North
Northern Bobwhite, *see* Bobwhite, Northern
Northern Flicker, *see* Flicker, Northern
Northern Goshawk, *see* Goshawk, Northern
Northern Harrier, *see* Harrier, Northern
Northern Mockingbird, *see* Mockingbird, Northern
Northern Pintail, *see* Pintail, Northern
Northern Rough-winged Swallow, *see* Swallow, Northern Rough-winged
Northern Saw-whet Owl, *see* Owl, Northern Saw-whet
Northern Shoveler, *see* Shoveler, Northern
Northern Shrike, *see* Shrike, Northern
Northern Waterthrush, *see* Waterthrush, Northern
Nussbaum, Louis Frédéric, 48
Nuthatch, Red-breasted, 231

Olive-sided Flycatcher, *see* Flycatcher, Olive-sided
Olliver, Bernice, **206**
Olswang, Mrs., 113
Orange-crowned Warbler, *see* Warbler, Orange-crowned
Oriole, Bullock's, 74, 234
Osprey, **215**, 225
Owl
  Barn, 228
  Barred, 189–192, 229
    photograph, **190**
  Great Horned, 229
  Northern Saw-whet, 229
  Short-eared, 228
  Snowy, 229
  Spotted, 191

Pacific Wren, *see* Wren, Pacific
Pacific-slope Flycatcher, *see* Flycatcher, Pacific-slope
Palm Warbler, *see* Warbler, Palm
Palmisano, Sam, 41–43
Parr, Tony, **214**
Parrott, Doug, 4, 11, 32, 40, 42, 54, **55**, 57, 64, 72, 89, 96, 109, 112, 117, 124, **136**, 139, 150, 166, 179, 187, 190, 198, 222, 227, **236**
Paulson Prairie, 45
Paulson, Dennis, **194**
Pectoral Sandpiper, *see* Sandpiper, Pectoral
Pelican, American White, 224
Peregrine Falcon, *see* Falcon, Peregrine
Peterson, Suzanne E., **216**
Pewee, Western Wood-, 229
Phalarope
  Red-necked, 228
    photograph, **205**
  Wilson's, 228
Pheasant, Ring-necked, 224
Phil, Dr., 161
Philosophy
  Alfred E. Neuman, 2
  Aristotle's definition of perfection, 148
  artistic perfection, 149
  constructed environment, 19
  cynicism all washed up, 78
  defining the good life, 84, 149, 157
  duality of reality, 38
  freedom of mind and spirit, 135
  give what you don't have, 25–26
  greatest strength/weakness, 2
  human limits, 91–92
  human rivalry, 40
  individuality vs. community, 196
  interconnectedness, 41, 84, 99, 145
  intersection of human and wild nature, 204
  joy in little things, 127
  money, 152–158
  nature of beauty, 57
  no limits to human achievement, 49
  purpose of cities, 145
  savor the moment, 7
  science and art, 181

Socrates's death, 168
survival of the fittest, 94
what you seek not far away, 90
widow's mite, 25
Phoebe
   Eastern, 47, 230
      photograph, **46**
   Say's, 74–77, 230
      photograph, **75**
Pied-billed Grebe, *see* Grebe, Pied-billed
Pigeon
   Band-tailed, 228
   Rock, 228
Pileated Woodpecker, *see* Woodpecker, Pileated
Pine Siskin, *see* Siskin, Pine
Pintail, Northern, 223
Pipit, American, 232
Plover
   American Golden-, 226
   Black-bellied, 226
   Semipalmated, 226
Poorwill, Common, 229
Purple Finch, *see* Finch, Purple
Purple Martin, *see* Martin, Purple
Puschock, John, 47

Quail, California, 224
Quartermaster Harbor, 66
Querencia, 122

Rail, Virginia, 17, 87, 150, 225
   photograph, **18**
Raven, Common, 230
Ravenholt, Lisa, 205, **206, 207**
Reading Rocks, 59
Recrudescence, 164
Red Crossbill, *see* Crossbill, Red
Red Pyramid, 82
Red-breasted Merganser, *see* Merganser, Red-breasted
Red-breasted Nuthatch, *see* Nuthatch, Red-breasted
Red-breasted Sapsucker, *see* Sapsucker, Red-breasted
Red-eyed Vireo, *see* Vireo, Red-eyed
Red-necked Grebe, *see* Grebe, Red-necked
Red-necked Phalarope, *see* Phalarope, Red-necked

Red-shouldered Hawk, *see* Hawk, Red-shouldered
Red-tailed Hawk, *see* Hawk, Red-tailed
Red-throated Loon, *see* Loon, Red-throated
Red-winged Blackbird, *see* Blackbird, Red-winged
Redhead, 223
Redpoll, Common, 234
Redstart, American, 233
"Reverence", **207**
Ring-billed Gull, *see* Gull, Ring-billed
Ring-necked Duck, *see* Duck, Ring-necked
Ring-necked Pheasant, *see* Pheasant, Ring-necked
Robin, American, 45, 58, 102, 232
   photograph, **104**
Rock Pigeon, *see* Pigeon, Rock
Rogers, Fred, 100
Rose-breasted Grosbeak, *see* Grosbeak, Rose-breasted
Ross's Goose, *see* Goose, Ross's
Rough-legged Hawk, *see* Hawk, Rough-legged
Ruby-crowned Kinglet, *see* Kinglet, Ruby-crowned
Ruddy Duck, *see* Duck, Ruddy
Ruff, 226
Rufous Hummingbird, *see* Hummingbird, Rufous
Run Silent, Run Deep, 34
Rusty Blackbird, *see* Blackbird, Rusty

Sage Sparrow, *see* Sparrow, Sage
Sage Thrasher, *see* Thrasher, Sage
Sale, Kirkpatrick, 122
Sanderling, 226
Sanders, Thomas, **97**, **143**, **162**, **201**
Sandes, Jane, 149, **215**
Sandhill Crane, *see* Crane, Sandhill
Sandpiper
   Baird's, 226
   Buff-breasted, 228
   Least, 184, 226
      photograph, **182**
   Pectoral, 226
   Semipalmated, 226
   Sharp-tailed, 226

Solitary, 71, 226
Spotted, 226
Stilt, 226
Upland, 226
Western, 226
Sapa Inca, 144
Sapsucker, Red-breasted, 229
Savannah Sparrow, *see* Sparrow, Savannah
Say's Phoebe, *see* Phoebe, Say's
Scaup
    Greater, 29, 223
        photograph, **32**
    Lesser, 29, 223
Schurman, Doug, **199**
Schwarzenegger, Arnold, 3
Schworer, Thomas, **206**
Scissor-tailed Flycatcher, *see* Flycatcher, Scissor-tailed
Scoter
    Surf, 223
    White-winged, 223
Secondhand Lions, 169
Secretariat, 49
Seki, Hiroko, **213**
Semipalmated Plover, *see* Plover, Semipalmated
Semipalmated Sandpiper, *see* Sandpiper, Semipalmated
Sharp-shinned Hawk, *see* Hawk, Sharp-shinned
Sharp-tailed Sandpiper, *see* Sandpiper, Sharp-tailed
Shearwater, Debi, 183
Short-billed Dowitcher, *see* Dowitcher, Short-billed
Short-eared Owl, *see* Owl, Short-eared
Shoveler's Pond, 71, **216**
    photograph, **101**
Shoveler's Pond, Winter, **212**
Shoveler, Northern, 223
    photograph, **158**
Shrike
    Loggerhead, 230
    Northern, 230
Sidles, Sheila, 186
Singles bars, 3–6
Siskin, Pine, 39–40, 44, 234
    photograph, **40**

Skimmer, Eight-spotted
    photograph, **194**
Slider, Red-eared
    photograph, **121**
Smith, Clineene, **206**
Smith, Huston, 192
Smith, Mary Lou, **101**, **209**
Sneferu, King, 81–82
Snipe, Wilson's, 88, 228
    photograph, **89**
Snow Bunting, *see* Bunting, Snow
Snow Goose, *see* Goose, Snow
Snowy Owl, *see* Owl, Snowy
Socrates, 168
Solitaire, Townsend's, 232
Solitary Sandpiper, *see* Sandpiper, Solitary
Song Sparrow, *see* Sparrow, Song
Sora, 71, 225
    photograph, **69**
South Bend, Indiana, 144
South Blue Forest, *see* Blue Forest, South
Southeast Pond, 87, 134
Southwest Pond, 17, 110, 160
    photograph, **151**
Sparrow
    American Tree, 233
    Black-throated, 233
    Brewer's, 233
    Chipping, 233
        photograph, **231**
    Clay-colored, 233
    Fox, 233
    Golden-crowned, 234
    Harris's, 233
    House, 235
    Lark, 233
    Lincoln's, 233
    Sage, 233
    Savannah, 233
    Song, 15–16, 23, 233
        photograph, **14**
    Swamp, 233
    Vesper, 233
    White-crowned, 233
    White-throated, 233
Spotted Sandpiper, *see* Sandpiper, Spotted
Spotted Towhee, *see* Towhee, Spotted

Sprague, Rachel, 218
Starling, European, 192, 232
Steller's Jay, see Jay, Steller's
Step Pyramid, 81
Stilt Sandpiper, see Sandpiper, Stilt
Stilt, Black-necked, 226
Surf Scoter, see Scoter, Surf
Swainson's Thrush, see Thrush, Swainson's
Swallow
  Bank, 231
  Barn, 147, 150, 159, 165, 231
    photograph, **150**
  Cliff, 130, 231
    photograph, **133**
  Northern Rough-winged, 231
  Tree, 231
  Violet-green, 231
Swamp Sparrow, see Sparrow, Swamp
Swan
  Mute, 223
  Trumpeter, 9–13, 223
    photograph, **8**, **11**
  Tundra, 223
Sweeney, Joe, **231**
Swift
  Black, 128–132, 229
    photograph, **129**
  Vaux's, 229

Tanager, Western, 233
Teal
  Blue-winged, 223
  Cinnamon, 223
  Eurasian, 223
  Green-winged, 223
Tennessee Warbler, see Warbler, Tennessee
Tepke, Glen, **129**
Tern
  Black, 228
  Caspian, 228
  Common, 228
Tevye, 193
Thayer's Gull, see Gull, Thayer's
Thompson, Gregg, **36**, **61**, **65**, **75**, **155**
Thrasher
  Brown, 232
  Sage, 232

Thrush
  Hermit, 232
  Swainson's, 232
  Varied, 232
Towhee, Spotted, 233
The Town, 59
Townsend's Solitaire, see Solitaire, Townsend's
Townsend's Warbler, see Warbler, Townsend's
Tree Swallow, see Swallow, Tree
Tropical Kingbird, see Kingbird, Tropical
Trumpeter Swan, see Swan, Trumpeter
Tufted Duck, see Duck, Tufted
Tundra Swan, see Swan, Tundra
Turkey Vulture, see Vulture, Turkey
Turtle Logs, 15, 196
Tutankhamun, King, 35–38
Tweedy, Penny, 49
Tweeters, 47, 108

UBNA, see Montlake Fill
Ulsh, Idie, **23**, **43**
Union Bay, 9, 13, 139, 176, 195, 205
Union Bay Natural Area, see Montlake Fill, **219**
University Slough, 116, 122, 140, 193
Upland Sandpiper, see Sandpiper, Upland

Varied Thrush, see Thrush, Varied
Varsity track, 80, 83
Vassallo, Collin, **28**
Vaux's Swift, see Swift, Vaux's
Vernon, Mark, 27–29
Vesper Sparrow, see Sparrow, Vesper
Violet-green Swallow, see Swallow, Violet-green
Vireo
  Blue-headed, 230
  Cassin's, 230
  Hutton's, 230
  Red-eyed, 230
  Warbling, 230
Virginia Rail, see Rail, Virginia
Vulture, Turkey, 170–172, **208**, 225
  photograph, **171**

Wahkiakum Lane, 45

photograph, **1**
Wallace, Geraldine, **206**
Warbler
    Black-throated Gray, 232
    MacGillivray's, 233
    Nashville, 232
    Orange-crowned, 71, 232
        photograph, **72**
    Palm, 233
    Tennessee, 232
    Townsend's, 232
    Wilson's, 233
    Yellow, 74, 232
    Yellow-rumped, 232
Warbling Vireo, *see* Vireo, Warbling
Washington Bird Records Committee, 64
Water Lily Cove, 9, 13, 184, 195
Waterthrush, Northern, 233
Waxwing, Cedar, 232
Western Grebe, *see* Grebe, Western
Western Gull, *see* Gull, Western
Western Kingbird, *see* Kingbird, Western
Western Meadowlark, *see* Meadowlark, Western
Western Sandpiper, *see* Sandpiper, Western
Western Scrub-Jay, *see* Jay, Western Scrub-
Western Tanager, *see* Tanager, Western
Western Wood-Pewee, *see* Pewee, Western Wood-
Wheeler, Woody, 191
Whimbrel, 226
White-crowned Sparrow, *see* Sparrow, White-crowned
White-throated Sparrow, *see* Sparrow, White-throated
White-winged Scoter, *see* Scoter, White-winged
Wigeon
    American, 195, 223
        photograph, **199**
    Eurasian, 223
Williams, Jackie, 205
Willow Flycatcher, *see* Flycatcher, Willow
Wilson's Phalarope, *see* Phalarope, Wilson's
Wilson's Snipe, *see* Snipe, Wilson's
Wilson's Warbler, *see* Warbler, Wilson's

Wittgenstein, Ludwig, 137
Women, union of, 5–6
Wood Duck, *see* Duck, Wood
Woodland Park Zoo, 171
Woodpecker
    Downy, 23, 229
    Hairy, 229
    Lewis's, 229
    Pileated, 229
Wren
    Bewick's, 232
    House, 232
    Marsh, 134, 232
        photograph, **136**, **139**
    Pacific, 23, 232

Yarrow, Judith, 217
Yeager, Sarah T., **212**
Yellow Warbler, *see* Warbler, Yellow
Yellow-headed Blackbird, *see* Blackbird, Yellow-headed
Yellow-rumped Warbler, *see* Warbler, Yellow-rumped
Yellowlegs
    Greater, 226
    Lesser, 226
Yellowthroat, Common, 141–142, 146, **210**, 233
    photograph, **143**
Yesler Cove, 9, 21, 191
Yesler Swamp, 13, 21, 57, 73, 154, 189
Young, Ricky, 183
Youth Farm, 45, 74

Zimmerman, Carleen Ormbrek, **219**